Fusion Math SAT + ACT Core Math Topics

By: Mark Batho and Gene Dennis

Contents

1	**Introduction**	2
2	**SAT & ACT Facts and Formulas**	3
3	**Example Problems**	8
4	**SAT + ACT MathPackets**	10
	4.1 Linear Equations	11
	4.2 Inequalities and Systems of Equations	16
	4.3 Ratios and Probability	22
	4.4 Radicals and Quadratic Equations Part 1	27
	4.5 Radicals and Quadratic Equations Part 2	32
	4.6 Exponents and Radicals	37
5	**SAT + ACT Packet Answers**	41
	5.1 Linear Equations Answers	42
	5.2 Inequalities and Systems of Equations Answers	44
	5.3 Ratios and Probability Answers	46
	5.4 Radicals and Quadratic Equations Part 1 Answers	47
	5.5 Radicals and Quadratic Equations Part 2 Answers	48
	5.6 Exponents and Radicals Answers	49

1 Introduction

Thanks for buying our SAT + ACT Core Math Topics book. Fusion Math is a Math and Science Tutoring Center in Seattle, WA. We have been tutoring the SAT and ACT for many years and have put together a collection of problems that we hope you will find engaging and useful in preparing for the SAT or ACT.

Our advice to you regarding the SAT, ACT, or any standardized test is to think a little about the best strategy on math problems before jumping into solving them. Many standardized math problems are often designed with two solutions in mind. The first and most obvious solution is usually a slower method but there is often a less obvious faster solution available for students that are well prepared. To complete a math section without running out of time, you need to use fast math methods rather than trying to do the math fast for this leads to errors.

Consider a math problem that asks the value of $x + y$. The most obvious way would seem to get the value of x, the value of y, and then add them. You should first consider if it is possible to solve for the value of $x + y$ directly, without ever solving for either variable.

The goal of any standardized test is to assess the math level of a student quickly. On the ACT for example, the test writers are given only 60 questions and 60 minutes to assess your entire 1st through 11th grade math education. That is a formidable task for them so let's talk about how they do that.

Initially they start out with very simple questions to give all students a chance to get some questions correct but fairly soon they move into more complex questions. Many of these more complex questions are attempting to answer two questions to the test writers. The first is simply whether can you solve the problem at all. The second questions is now well do you know the problem. If you know the problem well, you will likely find the fast method the test writers made for you. Answering questions with the a fast method will allow you to finish the section within the allotted time without rushing. Another method the test writers employ is to write problems that need to be solved in the opposite direction from what you are used to.

Here's an example of that: Instead of asking you what $(x - 7)^2$ is equal to, they will ask:

Which of the following is equivalent to $x^2 - 14x + 49$

A) $(x - 4)^2$
B) $(x - 9)^2$
C) $(x - 7)^2$
D) $(x + 7)^2$
E) $(x + 14)^2$

The correct answer is C). This questions requires knowing how to go backwards and essentially "undistribute" $x^2 - 14x + 49$ to get $(x - 7)^2$.

In this book we have created many problems that have both fast and slow solutions and ask many questions in "reverse". We suggest you work through the book on blank paper so you can rework the problems again without seeing your previous solution. Ask you friends, parents, and teachers for help. If you'd like some online tutoring please visit www.fusionmath.com. We also have videos at: www.youtube.com/fusionmath. Best of luck on your test!

2 SAT & ACT Facts and Formulas

Below you will find lists of Facts and Formulas that are useful to know when taking the SAT and ACT. Some formulas have been developed to answer specific question types on the SAT and ACT. We urge you to make flash cards with all the facts that you don't know yet and learn them well so you can put them into practice while doing the problems in this book as well as while taking SAT and ACT practice tests. For many extra SAT practice tests do a search on www.reddit.com with the keywords "QAS SAT."

1. Numbers and Number Properties
    - Natural Numbers: $\{1, 2, 3, \ldots\}$
    - Positive Integers: $\{1, 2, 3, \ldots\}$
    - Whole Numbers: $\{0, 1, 2, 3, \ldots\}$
    - Integers: $\{\ldots, -3, -2, -1, 0, 1, 2, 3, \ldots\}$
    - Zero is neither positive nor negative, but zero is even.
    - The smallest prime number is 2.

2. Times Tables up to 12x12 - Re-Learn them!
   Download "Fusion Math Fast Facts," our iOS Times Tables App from the App Store.

3. Special Numbers and Products
   $3 \cdot 16 = 48 \quad 4 \cdot 16 = 64 \quad 3 \cdot 17 = 51 \quad 12 \cdot 15 = 180$
   $3 \cdot 18 = 54 \quad 16 \cdot 9 = 144 \quad 3 \cdot 64 = 192 \quad 12 \cdot 16 = 192$
   $3 \cdot 14 = 42 \quad 7 \cdot 13 = 91 \quad \sqrt{2} \approx 1.41 \quad \sqrt{3} \approx 1.73$
   $5 \cdot 15 = 75 \quad 6 \cdot 15 = 90 \quad 7 \cdot 15 = 105 \quad 8 \cdot 18 = 144$

4. Squares up to 20^2
   $1^2 = 1 \quad 6^2 = 36 \quad 11^2 = 121 \quad 16^2 = 256$
   $2^2 = 4 \quad 7^2 = 49 \quad 12^2 = 144 \quad 17^2 = 289$
   $3^2 = 9 \quad 8^2 = 64 \quad 13^2 = 169 \quad 18^2 = 324$
   $4^2 = 16 \quad 9^2 = 81 \quad 14^2 = 196 \quad 19^2 = 361$
   $5^2 = 25 \quad 10^2 = 100 \quad 15^2 = 225 \quad 20^2 = 400$

5. Cubes up to 10^3
   $1^3 = 1 \quad 6^3 = 216$
   $2^3 = 8 \quad 7^3 = 343$
   $3^3 = 27 \quad 8^3 = 512$
   $4^3 = 64 \quad 9^3 = 729$
   $5^3 = 125 \quad 10^3 = 1000$

6. Fourth Powers up to 5^4
   $1^4 = 1$
   $2^4 = 16$
   $3^4 = 81$
   $4^4 = 256$
   $5^4 = 625$

7. Powers of 2 up to 2^{10}
   $2^1 = 2 \quad 2^6 = 64$
   $2^2 = 4 \quad 2^7 = 128$
   $2^3 = 8 \quad 2^8 = 256$
   $2^4 = 16 \quad 2^9 = 512$
   $2^5 = 32 \quad 2^{10} = 1024$

8. Know your Eighths!
    - $\frac{1}{8} = 0.125$
    - $\frac{2}{8} = \frac{1}{4} = 0.25$
    - $\frac{3}{8} = 0.375$
    - $\frac{4}{8} = \frac{1}{2} = 0.5$
    - $\frac{5}{8} = 0.625$
    - $\frac{6}{8} = \frac{3}{4} = 0.75$
    - $\frac{7}{8} = 0.875$

9. Special Angle Triangles:
    - $30°, 60°, 90°$ Side Ratios: $1 : \sqrt{3} : 2$ or $a : a\sqrt{3} : 2a$
    - $45°, 45°, 90°$ Side Ratios: $1 : 1 : \sqrt{2}$ or $a : a : a\sqrt{2}$

10. Pythagorean Triple Integer Right Triangles:
    - $3, 4, 5$ and multiples thereof such as $6, 8, 10$; $9, 12, 15$; $12, 16, 20$; $15, 20, 25$
    - $5, 12, 13$ and multiples thereof such as $10, 24, 26$
    - $8, 15, 17$ and multiples thereof such as $16, 30, 34$
    - $7, 24, 25$ and multiples thereof such as $14, 48, 50$

11. Geometry Formulas
    - Circumference of Circle: $C = 2\pi r$ or $C = \pi d$ where $d = 2r$
    - Area of Circle: $A = \pi r^2$ or $A = \frac{\pi}{4} d^2$ where $d = 2r$
    - Area of Sphere: $A = 4\pi r^2$ (4 times area of circle) or $A = \pi d^2$
    - Volume of Sphere: $V = \frac{4}{3}\pi r^3$
    - Length of Arc: $L = \frac{\theta}{360°}(2\pi r)$ where θ is central angle
    - Area of Sector of Circle: $A = \frac{\theta}{360°}(\pi r^2)$ where θ is central angle
    - Volume of All Prisms (Cylinder, Rectangular, Triangular, etc): $V = $ base area $\cdot$ height
    - Volume of Cone, Rectangular Pyramid, or Triangular Pyramid: $V = \frac{1}{3} \cdot$ base area $\cdot$ height
    - Area of Square: $A = $ (side length)^2
    - Area of Square: $A = \frac{(\text{diagonal})^2}{2}$
    - Area of Rectangle: $A = $ base $\cdot$ height
    - Area of Parallelogram: $A = $ base $\cdot$ height
    - Area of Trapezoid: $A = $ (average of bases) $\cdot$ height
    - Area of Triangle: $A = \frac{1}{2} \cdot$ base $\cdot$ height
    - Area of Kite: $A = \frac{1}{2} \cdot \text{diagonal}_1 \cdot \text{diagonal}_2$
    - Area of Equilateral Triangle: $\frac{\sqrt{3}}{4} \cdot$ (side length)^2
    - Area of Hexagon: $\frac{3\sqrt{3}}{2} \cdot$ (side length)^2
      or $\frac{3\sqrt{3}}{2} \cdot$ (distance from center to vertex)^2
    - 2-D Pythagoras: $a^2 + b^2 = c^2$ where c is the hypotenuse of the triangle

- 3-D Pythagoras: $a^2 + b^2 + c^2 = d^2$ where d is the diagonal of the rectangular solid (think cardboard box)
- If the Length Ratio of two similar shapes is $a : b$ or $\frac{a}{b}$, then the Area Ratio is $a^2 : b^2$ or $\frac{a^2}{b^2}$, and the Volume Ratio is $a^3 : b^3$ or $\frac{a^3}{b^3}$
  Example: If the ratio of the circumference of a smaller sphere to the circumference of a larger sphere is $1 : 2$ then the ratio of the area of the smaller sphere to the area of the larger sphere is $1^2 : 2^2$ or $1 : 4$ and the ratio of the volume of the smaller sphere to the volume of the larger sphere is $1^3 : 2^3$ or $1 : 8$.
- Sum of interior angles of n-sided polygon:
  $(n-2) \cdot 180°$ OR find the Exterior angle by dividing $360°$ by the number of vertices and then multiply ($180°$−exterior angle) by the number of vertices.
- Angle measure of one interior angle of an n-sided regular polygon: $180 - \frac{360°}{n}$

12. Function Formulas
    - Quadratic Standard Form: $y = ax^2 + bx + c$ where a, b, c are numbers or "constants"
    - Quadratic Formula: $\frac{-b}{2a} \pm \frac{\sqrt{b^2-4ac}}{2a}$ or $\frac{-b \pm \sqrt{b^2-4ac}}{2a}$
    - Quadratic Vertex Form: $y = a(x-h)^2 + k$ where (h, k) is the vertex of the parabola. Also note that: $h = \frac{-b}{2a}$
    - Line of symmetry of a quadratic function is $x = \frac{-b}{2a}$
    - The sum of the roots or zeros of a quadratic function is: $\frac{-b}{a}$
    - Cubic Formula: On TI-84 press APPS, then scroll to PLYSMLT2 and select. Then choose option 1, POLY ROOT FINDER and choose ORDER 3
    - Exponential Standard Form: $y = ab^x$ If given table of values always plug in the values where $x = 0$ so equation becomes $y = ab^0$ thus $y = a$ since $b^0 = 1$ Then plug in other values to solve for b.
    - Equation for Circle: $(x-h)^2 + (y-k)^2 = r^2$ where (h, k) is the center of the circle and r is the radius

13. Factoring Formulas
    - $(a+b)^2 = a^2 + 2ab + b^2$
      $(a-b)^2 = a^2 - 2ab + b^2$
      Rule: First term squared plus two times the product of the two terms plus second term squared)
    - $(x+a)(x+b) = x^2 + (a+b)x + (a \cdot b)$
    - $a^2 - b^2 = (a-b)(a+b)$
    - $a^2 - b = (a - \sqrt{b})(a + \sqrt{b})$, so $x^2 - 5 = (x - \sqrt{5})(x + \sqrt{5})$
    - $a^4 - b^4 = (a^2 - b^2)(a^2 + b^2) = (a-b)(a+b)(a^2+b^2)$
    - $\frac{a-b}{b-a} = -1$ or $(a-b) = -1(b-a)$

14. Distance / Speed / Time Formulas
    - If $d =$ distance and $t =$ time and $s =$ speed,
      $d = s \cdot t, s = \frac{d}{t}, t = \frac{d}{s}$
    - Average speed $= \frac{\text{total distance traveled}}{\text{total time}}$
    - If you drive/walk/run different speeds to and from a location (same distance each way) the average speed is NOT the average of the speeds, but a little less
      Average speed $= \frac{2 \cdot \text{speed}_1 \cdot \text{speed}_2}{\text{speed}_1 + \text{speed}_2} = \frac{2 \cdot s_1 \cdot s_2}{s_1 + s_2}$

15. Other Facts and Formulas
    - y is directly related to x **or** y varies directly as x **or** y is directly proportional to x is written as: $y = kx$ where k is a constant

- y is inversely related to x **or** y varies inversely as x **or** y is inversely proportional to x is written as: $y = \dfrac{k}{x}$ where k is a constant
- The slopes of perpendicular lines are opposite reciprocals. If $m = \dfrac{-2}{5}$, $m_\perp = \dfrac{5}{2}$ or $m_\perp = \dfrac{-1}{m}$
- The number of squares around the perimeter of an n by n gameboard will always be divisible by 4
- Even Function (y-axis symmetry):
  $f(-x) = f(x)$
- Odd Function (180° origin rotation symmetry):
  $f(-x) = -f(x)$
- The midpoint of (x_1, y_1) and (x_2, y_2) is simply:
  (average of x values, average of y values)
- Sum of a Sequence of Numbers: (first number + last number) · (amount of numbers ÷ 2) OR $\dfrac{n}{2}(a_1 + a_n)$
- $\dfrac{a+b}{c} = \dfrac{a}{c} + \dfrac{b}{c}$, so $\dfrac{x+y}{5} = \dfrac{x}{5} + \dfrac{y}{5}$
- $\dfrac{a+b+c}{d} = \dfrac{a}{d} + \dfrac{b}{d} + \dfrac{c}{d}$
- $\dfrac{1}{a} + \dfrac{1}{b} = \dfrac{a+b}{ab}$ example: $\dfrac{1}{3} + \dfrac{1}{5} = \dfrac{3+5}{3 \cdot 5} = \dfrac{8}{15}$
- Percent means "per century" so 4% means 4 per 100 so $\dfrac{4}{100}$ so 0.04
- If you are asked "What percent of 30 is 12?" you can translate it into math: "What" is your unknown (call it x), "percent" is per hundred, "of" is times, "is" means equals. So, x per hundred times 30 equals 12. Here's the equation: $\dfrac{x}{100} \cdot 30 = 12$
- Mean: Simply the average of a set of numbers
- Mode: Most common item (possible to have more than one mode)
- Median: Middle value if odd amount of numbers or average of middle two values if even amount of numbers

16. Problem Solving Advice (What to do when you don't know what to do)

    - Seriously, Dont panic! - Rather use strategies!
    - Write down everything that was given to you in abbreviated form.
        - Write down what each number represents. If a questions tells you that you end a process after three seconds, dont just write 3, write time = 3 seconds or just 3s.
        - If the numbers have units, include their units - Think about what these units imply - the units on one side of the equation HAVE to match the units on the other side of the equation.
    - If you're given or derive an equation, play around with it. See if you could get the equation in a form that looks more familiar.
    - Write down anything that is implied by the equation. For example does this question ask something about a circle? Then the standard equation for a circle may be useful.
    - Draw a picture of what's going on. If your initial impulse is to draw a graph, but you think there must be a faster way, there's probably not. Go with your impulses!
    - Look through the possible answers right away and see if there's an identifiable trend to the answers or if there's anything you could eliminate right away. Often 2 answers are obviously wrong and then it's down to the last two.
    - If you're not sure what type of equation to write for this problem, think about how you could write the problem as $y = mx + b$. Approx one third of the questions are based around linear equations.
    - If they give you a table of data, you should absolutely use it. If the problem is a grid-in, there's a high probability that your answer is something in that table.

- If the equation given is one that you don't fully grasp at first, a good starting place is plugging in values. Let's say you have a problem with $y = 1.08 \cdot 2^t$, create a table and plug in $t = 0$ and $t = 1$. See if anything pops out after that. With powers, always start with zero because it will drastically simplify the problem. Remember that any number to the power of zero equals 1.
- If after trying the points above you still don't see a path forward, mark the problem as one to revisit and come back to it. All the problems, regardless of difficulty are worth the same amount on the SAT or ACT
- One more thing... after finishing a problem but before choosing an answer, always re-read the last sentence of the question. This protects you from mis-remembering what the question was actually asking for.
  Example: Often a question will make a simple statement such as: $a - 2b$ and then will give you some other equation where it makes sense to solve for b. Then at the end the quesion will ask what the value of a is. When you get the answer for b you will likely see it in the answer choices and it's very tempting to choose it. But of course you need to double b to get a. This is a common trap that is easily avoided.

17. Divisibility Rules

    - Divisibility by 2: If a number is even, the number is divisible by 2.
    - Divisibility by 3: If the sum of a number's digits is divisible by 3, so is the number. Repeat as necessary.
      Example: Is 87504 divisible by 3? $8 + 7 + 5 + 0 + 4 = 24$ and 24 is divisible by 3, so 87504 is divisible by 3. We may continue and also add the digits of 24. $2 + 4 = 6$ and 6 is divisible by 3 so 87504 is divisible by 3.
    - Divisibility by 4: If the last two digits of a number form a new number that is divisible by 4, so is the original number.
      Example: 847465836 is divisible by 4 since 36 is divisible by 4.
    - Divisibility by 5: If a number ends in 5 or 0, the number is divisible by 5.
    - Divisibility by 6: If a number is even and divisible by 3, it is also divisible by 6 (see rule for 3 above).
    - Divisibility by 7: If the last digit of a number is doubled and subtracted from the number created by the remaining digits and the result is 0 or divisible by 7, so is the number. Repeat as necessary.
      Example: Is 7413 divisible by 7? Double the 3 to get 6. Subtract the 6 from 741 to get 735. Still can't tell? Repeat. Double the 5 to get 10. Subtract the 10 from 73 to get 63. 63 is divisible by 7, so 7413 is also divisible by 7.
    - Divisibility by 8: If the last three digits of a number form a new number that is divisible by 8, so is the original number.
      Example: 847465832 is divisible by 8 since 832 is divisible by 8.
    - Divisibility by 9: If the sum of a number's digits is divisible by 9, so is the number. Repeat as necessary.
      Example: Is 7210368 divisible by 9? $7 + 2 + 1 + 0 + 3 + 6 + 8 = 27$ and 27 is divisible by 9, so 7210368 is divisible by 9. We may continue and also add the digits of 27. $2 + 7 = 9$ and 9 is divisible by 9 so 7210368 is divisible by 9. Since 9 is divisible by 3, 7210368 is also divisible by 3.
    - Divisibility by 10: If a number ends in 0, the number is divisible by 10.
    - Divisibility by 11: Find the sum of every other digit. Find the sum of the remaining digits. Find the difference between these two sums. If the difference is 0 or divisible by 11, so is the original number.
      Example: Is 8075648372 divisible by 11? Add alternating digits: $8 + 7 + 6 + 8 + 7 = 36$. Now add the other alternating digits: $0 + 5 + 4 + 3 + 2 = 14$. Since $36 - 14 = 22$ and 22 is divisible by 11, 8075648372 is divisible by 11.

3 Example Problems

Example #1

Find the value of b that makes causes the following linear equations to have no solution:

$3x + -6y = 10$
$2x + by = 7$

The solution of a pair of linear equations (or other equations) occurs at the coordinates where their graphs intersect. For a pair of linear equations to have no solution the equations must not cross and this happens when they are parallel. This means the slopes must be the same.

If we solve both equations for y we can put both of them in $y = mx + b$ form and set the slopes equal to each other and solve for b.

Let's try it:

$$3x + -6y = 10$$
$$-6y = -3x + 10$$
$$y = \frac{-3x}{-6} + \frac{10}{-6}$$
$$y = \frac{-3}{-6}x - \frac{10}{6}$$
$$\text{slope, } m = \frac{-3}{-6} = \frac{3}{6} = \frac{1}{2}$$

$$2x + by = 7$$
$$by = -2x + 7$$
$$y = \frac{-2x}{b} + \frac{7}{b}$$
$$y = \frac{-2}{b}x + \frac{7}{b}$$
$$\text{slope, } m = \frac{-2}{b}$$

Now, we can equate slopes: $\frac{3}{6} = \frac{-2}{b}$ which we can cross multiply to get $3 \cdot b = 6 \cdot -2$ which gives $3b = -12$ and $b = -4$

Here's a **faster approach**: If you carefully analyze where the numbers for slope come from when solving the equation you will see that if an equation is written in $Ax + By = C$ form (also called Standard Form) that slope, $m = \frac{-A}{B}$. This is simply the opposite of the coefficient of x divided by the coefficient of y. If you memorize this fact you can quickly find the slope of a linear equation written in Standard Form. The slope of the first equation is then: $\frac{-(3)}{(-6)} = \frac{3}{6} = \frac{1}{2}$ and the slope of the second equation is: $\frac{-(2)}{(b)} = \frac{-2}{b}$. We can now equate the slopes and cross multiply the resuting expression $\frac{1}{2} = \frac{-2}{b}$ to get $1 \cdot b = 2 \cdot -2$ which gives $b = -4$.

But there is a third and **fastest approach**.

$3x + -6y = 10$
$2x + by = 7$

If we look at just the numbers in front of x and y we can actually cross multiply those numbers exactly as they are in the two equations when they are written above one another in Standard Form. We get: $3 \cdot b = 2 \cdot -6$ which again gives us $3b = -12$ and $b = -4$ very quickly. This method is derived from the knowledge of determinants of 2x2 matrices as they relate to linear equations.

Example #2

Given $3x - 6 = 17$ find the value of $x - 2$

The most obvious way to solve this equation is to simply solve for the value of x and then subtract 2.

Let's try it:

$$3x - 6 = 17 \quad \text{(given equation)}$$
$$3x = 23 \quad \text{(add 6 to both sides)}$$
$$x = \frac{23}{3} \quad \text{(divide both sides by 3)}$$
$$x - 2 = \frac{23}{3} - 2 \quad \text{(subtract 2 from both sides)}$$
$$x - 2 = \frac{23}{3} - \frac{2}{1} \quad \text{(rewrite 2 as a fraction)}$$
$$x - 2 = \frac{23}{3} - \frac{2 \cdot 3}{1 \cdot 3} \quad \text{(multiply numerator and denominator by 3 to create common denominators)}$$
$$x - 2 = \frac{23}{3} - \frac{6}{3} \quad \text{(simplify)}$$
$$x - 2 = \frac{23 - 6}{3} \quad \text{(simplify)}$$
$$x - 2 = \frac{17}{3} \quad \text{(simplify)}$$

The problem above could surely have been solved by doing some of the steps mentally but we have shown every small step because some students may choose to do the problem this way.

Now we will show two slightly different ways to do the problem much faster.

Factoring Method:

$$3x - 6 = 17 \quad \text{(given equation)}$$
$$3(x - 2) = 17 \quad \text{(factor out 3 from left side of equation)}$$
$$x - 2 = \frac{17}{3} \quad \text{(divide both sides by 3 to solve)}$$

Division Method:

$$3x - 6 = 17 \quad \text{(given equation)}$$
$$\frac{3x - 6}{3} = \frac{17}{3} \quad \text{(divide both sides by 3)}$$
$$\frac{3x}{3} - \frac{6}{3} = \frac{17}{3} \quad \text{(distribute division of 3 to each term in numerator)}$$
$$\frac{\cancel{3}x}{\cancel{3}} - 2 = \frac{17}{3} \quad \text{(simplify)}$$
$$x - 2 = \frac{17}{3} \quad \text{(solved)}$$

4 SAT + ACT MathPackets

Following are 6 Practice Sections that were developed to focus on key areas of both the SAT and ACT.

4.1 Linear Equations

Questions 1-5 refer to the following information. Students in a class observe the growth of a bamboo stalk over the course of a month and find its height could be estimated by the model

$$h = 2.7d + 8.1$$

where h is the height of the bamboo stalk in centimeters and d is the number of days after the student began observing.

1. Which of the following is the best interpretation of the number 8.1 in the model?
   A) The stalk grew 8.1 centimeters each day.
   B) The stalk grew 1 centimeter every 8.1 days.
   C) The stalk was 8.1 centimeters tall when the student began observing.
   D) The students observed the stalk for 8.1 days.

2. Which of the following is the best interpretation of the number 2.7 in the model?
   A) The stalk grew 2.7 centimeters each day.
   B) The stalk grew 1 centimeter every 2.7 days.
   C) The stalk was 2.7 centimeters tall when the student began observing.
   D) The students observed the stalk for 2.7 days.

3. Based on the model, which of the following is the best estimate, in centimeters, of the stalk's height 10 days after the student began observing?
   A) 3
   B) 11
   C) 27
   D) 35

4. Which of the following expresses the number of days d it took for the stalk to reach a height h?
   A) $d = \frac{h+8.1}{2.7}$
   B) $d = \frac{h-8.1}{2.7}$
   C) $d = 2.7h + 2.1$
   D) $d = 2.7h - 2.1$

5. Which of the following best represents the number of days it took for the stalk to reach a height of 27 centimeters?
   A) 5
   B) 7
   C) 10
   D) 12

Questions 6-10 refer to the following information. A popular car rental company's pricing follows the model

$$p = 0.4m + 18$$

where p is the price of renting the car in dollars and m is the distance driven in miles.

6. Write a sentence that properly interprets the number 0.4 in the model.

7. Write a sentence that properly interprets the number 18 in the model.

8. Based on the model, what is the price of renting a car and driving it for 70 miles?

9. Write an expression for m in terms of p.

10. Based on the model, if a customer was charged $78.80, how many miles did the customer drive?

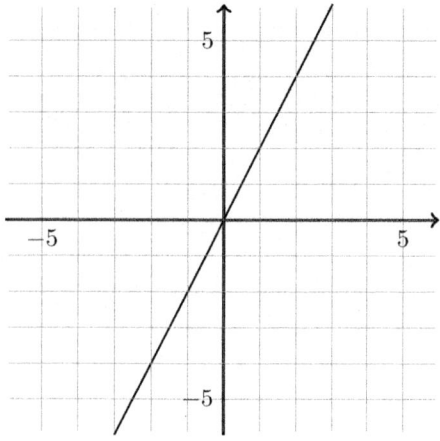

11. Write the equation for the graph above.

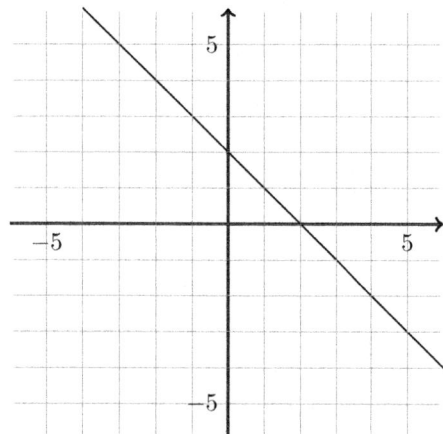

12. Write the equation for the graph above.

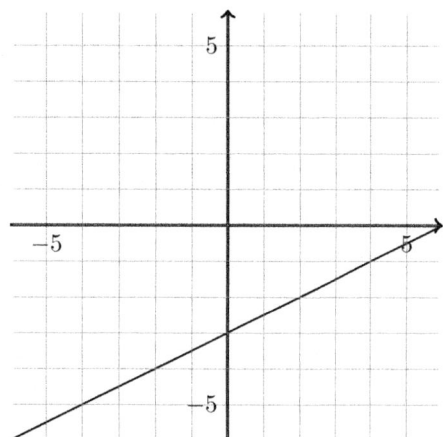

13. Write the equation for the graph above.

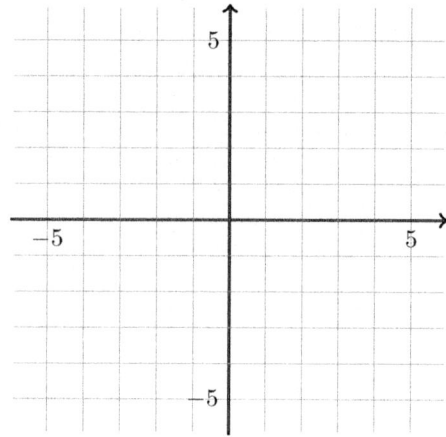

14. Sketch a graph for the equation $y = \frac{3}{2}x - 2$

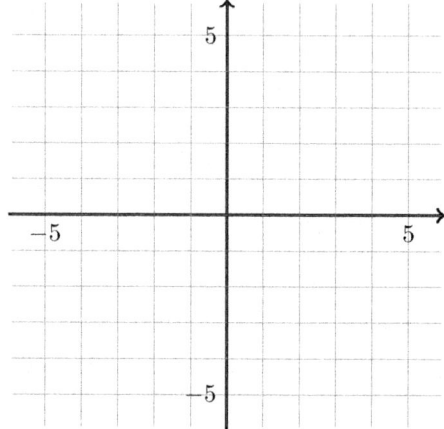

15. Sketch a graph for the equation $y = -\frac{x}{4} + 1$

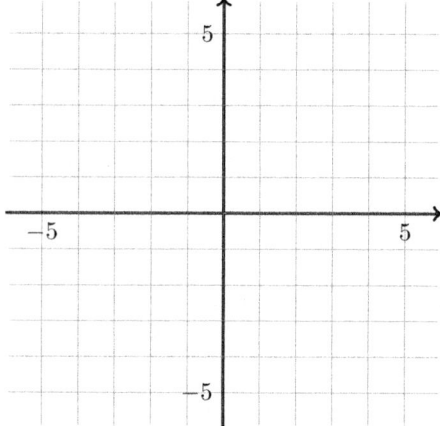

16. Sketch a graph for the equation $y = -\frac{2}{5}x - \frac{3}{5}$

Consider the graph of the equation

$$3x + 5y = 10$$

17. Which of the following best represents the slope of the line?
    A) 3
    B) −5
    C) $\frac{3}{5}$
    D) $\frac{-3}{5}$

18. Which of the following best represents the y-intercept of the graph?
    A) 2
    B) −5
    C) 5
    D) 10

19. Which of the following best represents the x-intercept of the graph?
    A) 3
    B) $\frac{10}{3}$
    C) $\frac{5}{3}$
    D) $\frac{3}{5}$

20. Which of the following points does NOT lie on the graph?
    A) $(-2, \frac{16}{5})$
    B) $(\frac{5}{3}, 1)$
    C) $(\frac{3}{5}, 3)$
    D) $(6, \frac{-8}{5})$

Consider the graph of the equation

$$4x + 6y = 12$$

21. Determine the slope of the graph.

22. Determine the y-intercept of the graph.

23. Determine the x-intercept of the graph.

Consider the graph of the equation

$$3y - 8x = 15$$

24. Determine the slope of the graph.

25. Determine the y-intercept of the graph.

26. Determine the x-intercept of the graph.

27. Which of the following points lies on the graph?
    A) $(3, -1)$
    B) $(-3, -3)$
    C) $(5, 1)$
    D) $(10, 2)$

Consider the graph of the equation

$$ax + by = c$$

where a, b and c are real constants.

28. Determine the slope of the graph.

29. Determine the y-intercept of the graph.

30. Determine the x-intercept of the graph.

Problems 31-38 refer to the following information.

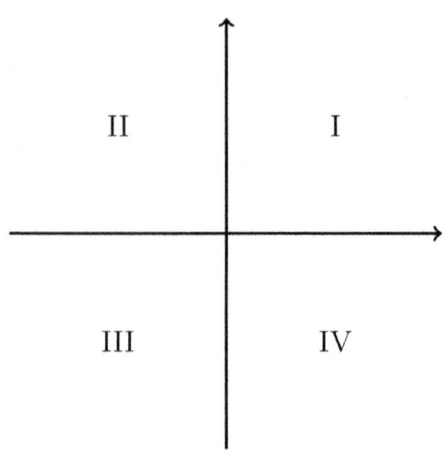

31. The graph of $y = 3x + 1$ in the xy-plane contains points from all quadrants EXCEPT
    A) I
    B) II
    C) III
    D) IV

32. The graph of $y = -2x + 4$ in the xy-plane contains points from all quadrants EXCEPT
    A) I
    B) II
    C) III
    D) IV

33. The graph of $y = -\frac{5}{2}x - 3$ in the xy-plane contains points from all quadrants EXCEPT
    A) I
    B) II
    C) III
    D) IV

34. The graph of $y = \frac{x}{4} - 5$ in the xy-plane contains points from all quadrants EXCEPT
    A) I
    B) II
    C) III
    D) IV

35. The graph of $3x - 4y = 16$ in the xy-plane contains points from all quadrants EXCEPT
    A) I
    B) II
    C) III
    D) IV

36. Line l in the xy-plane contains points from each of Quadrants I, II, and III but not Quadrant IV. Which of the following must be true?
    A) The slope of line l is undefined.
    B) The slope of line l is zero.
    C) The slope of line l is positive.
    D) The slope of line l is negative.

37. Line l in the xy-plane contains points from each of Quadrants I, III, and IV but not Quadrant II. Which of the following must be true?
    A) The y-intercept of line l is undefined.
    B) The y-intercept of line l is zero.
    C) The y-intercept of line l is positive.
    D) The y-intercept of line l is negative.

38. If the graph of an equation $y = ax + b$ in the xy-plane contains points from each of Quadrants I, II, and IV but not Quadrant III, which of the following must be true?
    A) $a > 0$, $b > 0$
    B) $a > 0$, $b < 0$
    C) $a < 0$, $b > 0$
    D) $a < 0$, $b < 0$

Consider line l, which has equation

$$y = \tfrac{2}{5}x - 1$$

39. Which of the following equations represents a line parallel to l?
    A) $y = \frac{5}{2}x - 1$
    B) $y = \frac{2}{5}x + 3$
    C) $y = -\frac{5}{2}x + 4$
    D) $y = -x + \frac{2}{5}$

40. Which of the following equations represents a line perpendicular to l?
    A) $y = \frac{5}{2}x - 1$
    B) $y = \frac{2}{5}x + 3$
    C) $y = -\frac{5}{2}x + 4$
    D) $y = -x + \frac{2}{5}$

Questions 41-42 refer to line l, which has equation

$$x - 4y = 9$$

41. Which of the following equations represents a line parallel to l?
    A) $3x - 4y = 9$
    B) $x - 12y = 9$
    C) $3x - 12y = 9$
    D) $3x + 12y = 9$

42. Which of the following equations represents a line perpendicular to l?
    A) $4x - y = 6$
    B) $8x - 2y = 18$
    C) $12x + 3y = -1$
    D) $2x - 8y = 4$

Questions 43-44 refer to line l, which has equation

$$2x + 4y + 7 = 0$$

43. Which of the following equations represents a line parallel to l?
    A) $x + 2y = 4$
    B) $2x - 4y = 3$
    C) $3x - 6y = -7$
    D) $4x + 2y = 0$

44. Which of the following equations represents a line perpendicular to l?
    A) $4x + 2y + 7 = 0$
    B) $4x - 2y + 3 = 0$
    C) $4x - y + 9 = 0$
    D) $7x + 2y + 4 = 0$

Question 45 refers to line l, which has equation

$$ax + by = c$$

where a, b, and c are real constants.

45. Line l is parallel to the lines represented by all of the following equations EXCEPT
    A) $3ax + 3by = 7$
    B) $5ax + 5by = c$
    C) $ax - by = -c$
    D) $x + \frac{b}{a}y = c$

Question 46 refers to line l, whose graph is shown below.

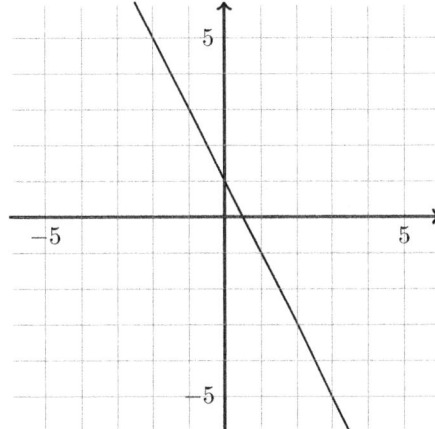

46. Which of the following represents a line parallel to l?
    A) $2x - 3y = 4$
    B) $2x + y = 4$
    C) $x - 2y = 4$
    D) $x + 2y = 4$

4.2 Inequalities and Systems of Equations

Questions 1-3 refer to the following inequality

$$3x - 2 < 5x + 4$$

1. Which of the following is a solution to the above inequality?
   A) -1
   B) -3
   C) -5
   D) -7

2. Which of the following is NOT a solution to the above inequality?
   A) 2
   B) 0
   C) -2
   D) -4

3. Which of the following inequalities is equivalent to the inequality above? (Note: this means the same thing as "solve the inequality")
   A) $x > 3$
   B) $x < 3$
   C) $x > -3$
   D) $x < -3$

Questions 4-5 refer to the following inequality

$$2(4-x) - 3x \geq -2$$

4. Which of the following is a solution to the above inequality?
   A) 5
   B) 4
   C) 3
   D) 2

5. Which of the following inequalities is equivalent to the inequality above?
   A) $x \geq 2$
   B) $x \leq 2$
   C) $x \geq -2$
   D) $x \leq -2$

$$\frac{8}{x} - 3 < 1$$

6. Which of the following inequalities is NOT a solution to the above inequality?
   A) 5
   B) 4
   C) 3
   D) 2

7. Which of the following inequalities is equivalent to the inequality above?
   A) $x > 2$
   B) $x < 2$
   C) $x > 2$ or $x < 0$
   D) $x < 2$ or $x > 0$

$$4x + 7 - 3(1 - 2x) > -2$$

8. Solve the inequality above.

$$\frac{4}{2-x} < -3$$

9. Carefully solve the inequality above.

$$\frac{1}{2x+4} \geq 2$$

10. Carefully solve the inequality above.

$$3x - 2y < 6$$

11. Which of the following ordered pairs (x, y) is a solution to the inequality above?
    A) $(3, 0)$
    B) $(0, 2)$
    C) $(2, 0)$
    D) $(1, -2)$

12. Which of the following inequalities is equivalent to the inequality above?
    A) $y > \frac{3}{2}x + 3$
    B) $y < \frac{3}{2}x + 3$
    C) $y > \frac{3}{2}x - 3$
    D) $y < \frac{3}{2}x - 3$

13. If $y = 1$ in the inequality above, which of the following best represents the solutions to the inequality? (Note: this means the same thing as "solve the inequality for $y = 1$")
    A) $x > 2$
    B) $x < 2$
    C) $x > \frac{8}{3}$
    D) $x < \frac{8}{3}$

$$x + 4y \geq -12$$

14. Which of the following ordered pairs (x, y) is NOT a solution to the inequality above?
    A) $(-1, 2)$
    B) $(-4, -2)$
    C) $(2, -5)$
    D) $(5, -4)$

15. Which of the following ordered pairs (x, y) satisfies the inequality above?
    A) $(0, 0)$
    B) $(-2, -4)$
    C) $(-1, -3)$
    D) $(4, -5)$

$$2y - 6x > 12$$

16. Solve the inequality above for y.

17. Solve the inequality above for x.

18. Solve the inequality above for y if $x = -1$.

19. Solve the inequality above for x if $y = 2$.

$$ax + by \leq c$$

where a, b, and c are real constants.

20. Solve the inequality above for y if $b > 0$.

21. Solve the inequality above for x if $a < 0$.

22. Solve the inequality above for y if $x = 5$ and $b < 0$.

23. Carefully solve the inequality above for y if $ax \geq 2$ and $b > 0$.

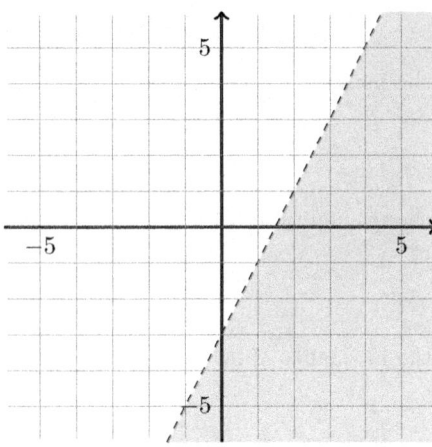

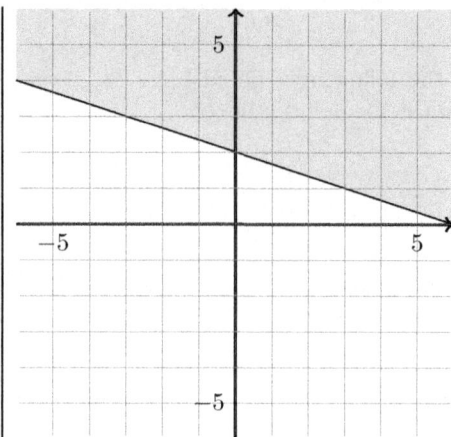

24. Which of the following inequalities best describes the graph above?
    A) $y \geq 2x - 3$
    B) $y \leq 2x - 3$
    C) $y > 2x - 3$
    D) $y < 2x - 3$

25. Which of the following ordered pairs is a solution to the inequality represented by the graph above?
    A) $(3, 5)$
    B) $(0, 0)$
    C) $(2, 0)$
    D) $(0, 3)$

27. Which of the following inequalities best describes the graph above?
    A) $3y + x \geq 2$
    B) $3y - x \geq 2$
    C) $3y + x \geq 6$
    D) $3y - x \geq 6$

28. Which of the following ordered pairs is NOT a solution to the inequality presented by the graph above?
    A) $(0, 2)$
    B) $(2, 1)$
    C) $(5, \frac{1}{2})$
    D) $(-3, 4)$

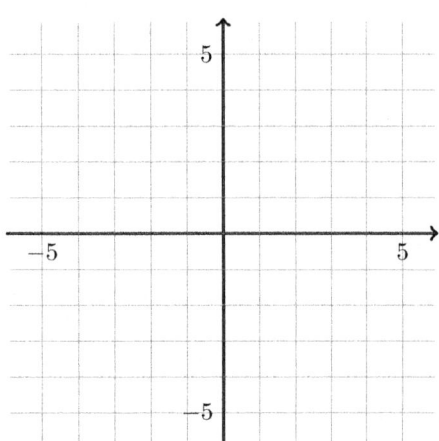

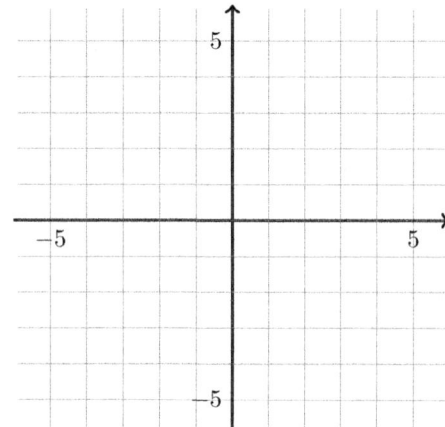

26. In the space above, sketch a graph of
$$y > -3x + 1$$

29. In the space above, sketch a graph of
$$2x - 3y \leq -1$$

18

$$y = 3x - 2$$
$$y = -2x + 8$$

30. Which of the following ordered pairs (x, y) is a solution to the system of equations above?
    A) $(1, 3)$
    B) $(2, 4)$
    C) $(3, 1)$
    D) $(4, 2)$

31. For the solution (x, y) to the system of equations above, what is the value of $2y - x$?
    A) 10
    B) 8
    C) 6
    D) 4

$$5x + 2y = -1$$
$$3x - 4y = 15$$

32. Find the solution (x, y) to the system of equations above.

$$4x + 7y = 12$$
$$3x + 6y = 7$$

33. For the solution (x, y) to the system of equations above, what is the value of $x + y$?

$$3x - 5y = -3$$
$$x + y = 4$$

34. For the solution (x, y) to the system of equations above, what is the value of $4x - 4y$?

$$5x + y = 7$$
$$3x - y = 3$$

35. For the solution (x, y) to the system of equations above, what is the value of $x + y$?

$$2x - 6y = -5$$
$$2x + 2y = 1$$

36. For the solution (x, y) to the system of equations above, what is the value of $x - y$?

$$4x + 2y = 12$$
$$-y + 7x = -3$$

37. For the solution (x, y) to the system of equations above, what is the value of $x - y$?

$$-2y + 3x = 4$$
$$6x + y = 6$$

38. For the solution (x, y) to the system of equations above, what is the value of $x + y$?

$$2y - x = 17$$
$$y - 2x = 4$$

39. For the solution (x, y) to the system of equations above, what is the value of $x - y$?

$$y = 3x + 2$$
$$y = 3x + 5$$

40. How many solutions (x, y) are there to the system of equations above?
    A) Zero
    B) One
    C) Two
    D) More than two

$$y = -2x + 4$$
$$y = 4x - 2$$

41. How many solutions (x, y) are there to the system of equations above?
    A) Zero
    B) One
    C) Two
    D) More than two

$$3x - 2y = 6$$
$$6x - 4y = 12$$

42. How many solutions (x, y) are there to the system of equations above?
    A) Zero
    B) One
    C) Two
    D) More than two

$$8x - 5y = -2$$
$$-3y + 4x = -1$$

43. How many solutions (x, y) are there to the system of equations above?
    A) Zero
    B) One
    C) Two
    D) More than two

$$3x + 5y = -4$$
$$9x + 15y = -12$$

44. How many solutions (x, y) are there to the system of equations above?
    A) Zero
    B) One
    C) Two
    D) More than two

$$9x - 6y = 8$$
$$3x - 2y = 4$$

45. How many solutions (x, y) are there to the system of equations above?
    A) Zero
    B) One
    C) Two
    D) More than two

$$5x - 3y = 8$$
$$5x + ay = b$$

46. If there are infinitely many solutions $(x.y)$ to the system of equations above, what are the values of a and b?

$$3x + ay = 10$$
$$bx + 8y = 20$$

47. If there are infinitely many solutions (x, y) to the system of equations above, what are the values of a and b?

$$ax - 4y = 9$$
$$bx + 4y = -9$$

48. If there are infinitely many solutions (x, y) to the system of equations above, what is the value of $a + b$?
    A) 4
    B) 2
    C) 0
    D) −4

$$2x + ay = 6$$
$$3x - by = 9$$

49. If there are zero solutions (x, y) to the system of equations above, what could be the value of $\frac{a}{b}$?
    A) $\frac{4}{3}$
    B) $\frac{-2}{3}$
    C) 0
    D) -4

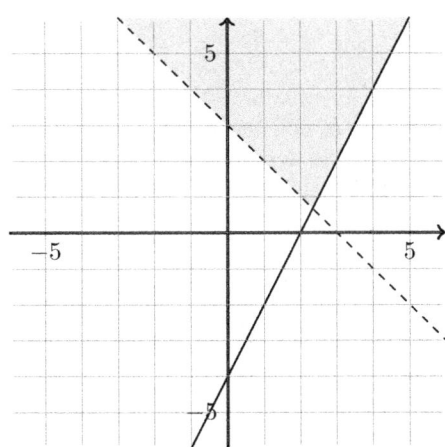

50. Which of the following systems of inequalities best describes the graph above?
    A) $y \geq -x + 3$
       $y > 2x - 4$
    B) $y > -x + 3$
       $y \geq 2x - 4$
    C) $y > -x + 3$
       $y \leq 2x - 4$
    D) $y \geq -x + 3$
       $y \geq 2x - 4$

51. Which of the following ordered pairs (x, y) is NOT a solution to the system of inequalities represented by the graph above?
    A) (0,4)
    B) (3,7)
    C) (2,1)
    D) (3,2)

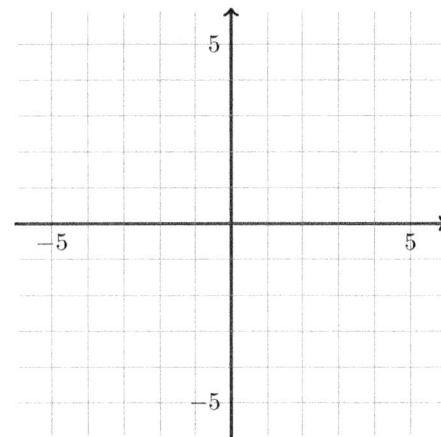

52. In the space above, sketch a graph of the solution to the system
$$2x + y < 3$$
$$3x - y \leq -2$$

Questions 53-55 rely on the system of inequalities below.
$$3x + 4y > a$$
$$5x - 2y < b$$

53. If $(0, 0)$ is a solution to the system of inequalities, which of the following must be true?
    A) $a < b$
    B) $a > b$
    C) $a = b$
    D) $|a| > |b|$

54. If $(1, -1)$ is a solution to the system of inequalities, which of the following must be true?
    A) $a < b$
    B) $a > b$
    C) $a = b$
    D) $|a| > |b|$

55. If $(1, 1)$ is a solution to the system of inequalities, which of the following CANNOT be true?
    A) $a < b$
    B) $a > b$
    C) $a = 0$
    D) $b = 0$

4.3 Ratios and Probability

1. If $\frac{a}{b} = 3$ and $b = 7$, what is the value of a?
   A) 3
   B) $\frac{3}{7}$
   C) $\frac{7}{3}$
   D) 21

2. If $\frac{a}{b} = 4$, what is the value of $\frac{3b}{a}$?
   A) $\frac{4}{3}$
   B) $\frac{3}{4}$
   C) $\frac{1}{12}$
   D) 12

3. If $\frac{a}{b} = \frac{3}{2}$, what is the value of $\frac{a+b}{b}$?
   A) $\frac{3}{2}$
   B) 2
   C) $\frac{5}{2}$
   D) 3

4. If $\frac{a-b}{b} = 3$, what is the value of $\frac{a}{b}$?
   A) 1
   B) 2
   C) 3
   D) 4

5. If $\frac{a+4}{5-a} = 2$, what is the value of a?
   A) 2
   B) $\frac{1}{2}$
   C) 0
   D) -2

6. If $\frac{2a+b}{c} = \frac{5}{2}$ and $\frac{c}{a} = 4$, what is the value of $\frac{b}{c}$?
   A) 2
   B) 3
   C) 4
   D) 5

7. If $\frac{3a-b}{c} = 1$ and $\frac{b}{a} = 2$, what is the value of $\frac{c}{b}$?
   A) 0
   B) $\frac{1}{2}$
   C) 1
   D) 2

8. Alan runs 1.5 miles in 10 minutes. At the same pace, how long will it take him to run 12 miles?

9. Denise paints 35 identically sized sections of a fence in 3 hours. At the same rate, how long will it take her to paint 14 sections of the fence?

10. A cookie recipe calls for $1\frac{1}{2}$ cups of brown sugar for every 1 cup of powder sugar. If we add 4 cups of brown sugar, how many cups of powder sugar should we add to satisfy the recipe?

11. In the US, a fluid ounce is $\frac{1}{16}$ of a fluid pint and a fluid pint is approximately 480 milliliters. What is the approximate volume, in milliliters, of a 12 fluid ounce cup?

12. The ratio of blue marbles to yellow marbles in a bag is 7:5. If the number of yellow marbles is 18 less than twice the number of blue marbles, how many marbles are in the bag?

13. If y is 30% of x, which of the following equations best represents the relationship between x and y?
    A) $y = 30x$
    B) $y = 0.3x$
    C) $x/0.3$
    D) $0.3/x$

14. If y is the result of increasing the value of x by 40%, which of the following equations best represents the relationship between x and y?
    A) $y = 0.4x$
    B) $y = x + 0.4$
    C) $x/0.4$
    D) $y = 1.4x$

15. If y is the result of decreasing the value of x by 25%, which of the following equations best represents the relationship between x and y?
    A) $y = 0.25x$
    B) $y = x - 0.25$
    C) $x/0.25$
    D) $y = 0.75x$

Two factories A and B produce widgets of the same model. Data show that 5% of widgets produced at factory A are defective and 8% of widgets produced at factory B are defective. Let a represent the number of widgets produced at factory A and b represent the number of widgets produced at factory B.

16. Which of the following equations is the best representation of D, the total number of defective widgets produced by factories A and B?
    A) $D = 5a + 8b$
    B) $D = 0.5a + 0.8b$
    C) $D = 0.05a + 0.08b$
    D) $D = 0.13(a + b)$

17. Which of the following equations is the best representation of R, the proportion of of the total widgets produced by factories A and B that are defective?
    A) $R = \frac{0.05a + 0.08b}{a+b}$
    B) $R = \frac{0.05 + 0.08}{2}$
    C) $R = \frac{0.05a - 0.08b}{a-b}$
    D) $R = \frac{0.05a + 0.08b}{2}$

For the holiday season, a department store is offering a 24% discount off all its clothing merchandise and a 17% discount off all its electronics merchandise. Sales tax is 8%. For any given shopping cart, let C be the total orginal retail price of the clothing items and E be the total original retail price of the electronics items.

18. If a shopping cart contains only clothing items, which of the following is the best representation of the final price, including tax?
    A) $0.16C$
    B) $0.84C$
    C) $(1.08)(0.76)C$
    D) $\frac{1.08}{1.24}C$

19. If a shopping cart contains only electronics items and p is the final price, including tax, which of the following is the best representation of E?
    A) $(1.08)(1.17)p$
    B) $(1.09)p$
    C) $\frac{1.17}{1.08}p$
    D) $\frac{p}{(1.08)(0.83)}$

20. If a shopping cart contains both clothing and electronics items, which of the following is the best representation of the total effective discount rate, not including tax?
    A) 0.205
    B) $\frac{0.24C + 0.17E}{C+E}$
    C) $\frac{0.24C + 0.17E}{2}$
    D) $\frac{0.76C + 0.83E}{C+E}$

21. A customer has a $300 shopping budget and wants to purchase jackets that originally cost $25 each. What is the maximum number of jackets this customer can purchase during the holiday sale at this department store?
    A) 11
    B) 12
    C) 13
    D) 14

A class of 50 students is asked what musical instruments they play. The results indicate that 18 students play string instruments, 27 students play band instruments, and 12 students play no instrument.

22. What percent of the students in the class play no instrument?
    A) 6%
    B) 12%
    C) 24%
    D) 50%

23. What percent of the students in the class play both string and band instruments?
    A) 14%
    B) 36%
    C) 54%
    D) 90%

24. What percent of the students in the class play at least one instrument?
    A) 72%
    B) 76%
    C) 88%
    D) 100%

25. What percent of the students in the class play only one type (string or band) of instrument?
    A) 14%
    B) 48%
    C) 62%
    D) 76%

26. Of the students who play a band instrument, approximately what percent play only a band instrument?
    A) 42%
    B) 54%
    C) 74%
    D) 100%

27. Of the students in the class who play a string instrument, approximately what percent also play a band instrument?
    A) 14%
    B) 26%
    C) 36%
    D) 39%

A survey of 96 high school sophomores showed that 68.75% planned to take the SAT, 43.75% planned to take the ACT, and 18.75% planned to take both.

28. Of the students in the class who play at least one instrument, approximately what percent play only a string instrument?
    A) 22%
    B) 29%
    C) 36%
    D) 47%

29. How many students planned to take the SAT?

30. How many students planned to take the ACT?

31. How many students planned to take both the SAT and the ACT?

32. How many students planned to take the SAT or the ACT?

33. How many students planned to take only the ACT?

34. How many students planned to take neither the SAT nor the ACT?

35. The number of students who planned to take only the SAT was what percent greater than the number of students who planned to take only the ACT?

36. The number of students who planned to take both the SAT and the ACT is what percent of the students who planned on taking neither the SAT not the ACT?

Consider two six-sided dice with faces numbered 1 through 6. One die is red and the other is yellow. The dice are rolled simultaneously and the value of each die is given by the number on its top face.

37. What is the probability that the red die is even?
    A) $\frac{1}{6}$
    B) $\frac{1}{4}$
    C) $\frac{1}{3}$
    D) $\frac{1}{2}$

38. What is the probability that both dice are even?
    A) $\frac{1}{6}$
    B) $\frac{1}{4}$
    C) $\frac{1}{3}$
    D) $\frac{1}{2}$

39. What is the probability that at least one of the dice is odd?
    A) $\frac{1}{4}$
    B) $\frac{1}{2}$
    C) $\frac{3}{4}$
    D) $\frac{5}{6}$

40. What is the probability that the sum of the dice is 2?
    A) $\frac{1}{36}$
    B) $\frac{1}{18}$
    C) $\frac{1}{6}$
    D) $\frac{1}{2}$

41. What is the probability that the difference of the dice is 4?
    A) $\frac{1}{36}$
    B) $\frac{1}{9}$
    C) $\frac{1}{6}$
    D) $\frac{1}{4}$

A deck of cards contains 4 suits (clubs, diamonds, hearts and spades) of 13 cards each (numbered 2 through 10, Jack, Queen, King and Ace).

42. If a card is drawn at random from a full deck, what is the probability of drawing a club or a heart?

43. If a card is drawn at random from a full deck, what is the probability that the card will be a club and a face card (Jack, Queen, King, or Ace)?

44. If a card is drawn at random from a full deck, what is the probability that the card will be a club or a face card (Jack, Queen, King, or Ace)?

45. If a card is drawn at random from a full deck, what is the probability that the card will be neither a club nor a face card (Jack, Queen, King or Ace)?

46. If a card is drawn at random from a full deck. Given the card is a face card (Jack, Queen, King or Ace), what is the probability that the card is a Queen?

47. A card is drawn at random from a full deck. Given the card is not a face card, what is the probability that the card is the 7 of hearts?

Math and Science Class Enrollment for Seniors in 2017

Math class	Science Class			
	Biology	Chemistry	Physics	Total
Precalculus	28	40	10	78
Calculus	23	16	35	74
Total	51	56	45	152

The table above represents the math and science classes taken by high school seniors at a particular high school in 2017.

48. What proportion of seniors are enrolled in Calculus?
    A) $\dfrac{23}{51}$
    B) $\dfrac{16}{56}$
    C) $\dfrac{35}{45}$
    D) $\dfrac{74}{152}$

49. What proportion of seniors are enrolled in Chemistry?
    A) $\dfrac{40}{78}$
    B) $\dfrac{16}{74}$
    C) $\dfrac{56}{152}$
    D) $\dfrac{40}{56}$

50. What proportion of seniors enrolled in Physics are also enrolled in Precalculus?
    A) $\dfrac{10}{51}$
    B) $\dfrac{10}{45}$
    C) $\dfrac{10}{78}$
    D) $\dfrac{10}{152}$

51. What proportion of seniors enrolled in Calculus are not enrolled in Biology?
    A) $\dfrac{23}{51}$
    B) $\dfrac{23}{74}$
    C) $\dfrac{51}{74}$
    D) $\dfrac{51}{152}$

Voter Party Identification by Age in Precinct X

Age	Party Identification			
	Democrat	Republican	Other	Total
18 to 25	40	57	12	109
26 to 35	122	88	35	245
36 to 45	72	65	18	155
46 to 55	53	63	8	124
56+	34	62	2	98
Total	321	335	75	731

The table above shows the results of a random survey of 731 voters in Precinct X, sorted by age range and party identification.

52. What proportion of the survey respondents identified themselves as Republican?

53. What proportion of the survey respondents were age 35 or younger?

54. What proportion of the survey respondents were age 46 or older and identified themselves as Democrat?

55. What proportion of the survey respondents who identified themselves as Democrat were age 46 or older?

56. What proportion of the survey respondents age 36 to 45 identified themselves as Other?

4.4 Radicals and Quadratic Equations Part 1

1. Which of the following is equivalent to $(x+a)^2$?
   A) $x^2 + a^2$
   B) $x^2 - a^2$
   C) $x^2 + 2ax + a^2$
   D) $x^2 - 2ax + a^2$

2. Which of the following is equivalent to $(x-a)^2$?
   A) $x^2 + a^2$
   B) $x^2 - a^2$
   C) $x^2 + 2ax - a^2$
   D) $x^2 - 2ax + a^2$

3. Which of the following is equivalent to $(x+a)(x-a)$?
   A) $x^2 + a^2$
   B) $x^2 - a^2$
   C) $x^2 + 2ax + a^2$
   D) $x^2 - 2ax - a^2$

4. Which of the following is equivalent to $(2a - \frac{b}{4})^2$?
   A) $2a^2 + \frac{b^2}{4}$
   B) $4a^2 + \frac{b^2}{16}$
   C) $4a^2 - \frac{ab}{2} + \frac{b^2}{16}$
   D) $4a^2 - ab + \frac{b^2}{16}$

$$(x+a)(x+b) = x^2 + cx + d$$

5. If the equation above is true for all values of x, which of the following must be the value of c?
   A) a
   B) b
   C) $a+b$
   D) ab

6. If the equation above is true for all values of x, which of the following must be the value of d?
   A) a
   B) b
   C) $a+b$
   D) ab

7. If the equation above is true for all values of x, a and b are integers, and $d = -15$, which of the following CANNOT be the value of c?
   A) 14
   B) 2
   C) -2
   D) -15

$$9x^2 - 1 = (ax+b)(ax-b)$$

8. If the equation above is true for all values of x, which of the following could be the value of a?
   A) 9
   B) 3
   C) 1
   D) 0

9. If the equation above is true for all values of x, which of the following could be the value of b?
   A) 9
   B) 3
   C) 1
   D) 0

$$\tfrac{1}{4}(25x^2 - 9) = (ax+b)(ax-b)$$

10. If the equation above is true for all values of x, which of the following could be the value of a?
    A) 25
    B) 5
    C) $\frac{5}{4}$
    D) $-\frac{5}{2}$

11. If the equation above is true for all values of x, which of the following could be the value of b?
    A) 9
    B) 3
    C) $\frac{3}{4}$
    D) $-\frac{3}{2}$

$$4x^2 - 4ax + 25 = (2x+b)^2$$

12. If the equation above is true for all values of x, which of the following could be the value of b?
    A) 25
    B) 5
    C) $\frac{5}{4}$
    D) $\frac{5}{2}$

13. If the equation above is true for all values of x, which of the following could be the value of a?
    A) 25
    B) 5
    C) $\frac{5}{4}$
    D) $\frac{5}{2}$

14. Which of the following is equivalent to $5 + \sqrt{2} - (3 - 2\sqrt{2})$?
    A) $2 - \sqrt{2}$
    B) $2 + 3\sqrt{2}$
    C) $5\sqrt{2}$
    D) $\sqrt{2}$

15. Which of the following is equivalent to $(\sqrt{2} + \sqrt{3})^2$?
    A) 5
    B) $5 + \sqrt{6}$
    C) $5 + 2\sqrt{6}$
    D) $5 + 2\sqrt{5}$

16. Which of the following is equivalent to $(4 + \sqrt{5})(4 - \sqrt{5})$?
    A) 11
    B) -9
    C) -1
    D) $21 - 8\sqrt{5}$

17. Which of the following is equivalent to $\frac{6}{\sqrt{3}}$?
    A) 2
    B) $2\sqrt{3}$
    C) $6\sqrt{3}$
    D) $\sqrt{2}$

18. Which of the following is equivalent to $\frac{2}{3-\sqrt{5}}$?
    A) $\frac{2}{3} - \frac{2}{5}\sqrt{5}$
    B) $\frac{3}{2} - \frac{2}{5}\sqrt{5}$
    C) $\frac{2}{3} + \frac{1}{2}\sqrt{5}$
    D) $\frac{3}{2} + \frac{1}{2}\sqrt{5}$

19. Which of the following is equivalent to $\frac{3-\sqrt{2}}{3+\sqrt{2}}$?
    A) $\frac{11}{7} - \frac{6}{7}\sqrt{2}$
    B) $\frac{11}{7} + \frac{6}{7}\sqrt{2}$
    C) 1
    D) -1

20. What is the sum of the complex numbers $3 + 2i$ and $5 + 6i$, where $i = \sqrt{-1}$?
    A) 16
    B) 0
    C) $8 + 8i$
    D) $15 + 12i$

21. Which of the following is equivalent to $(4 - 3i)^2$, where $i = \sqrt{-1}$?
    A) 25
    B) 7
    C) $25 - 24i$
    D) $7 - 24i$

22. Which of the following is equivalent to $(\sqrt{2} + 2i)(\sqrt{2} - 2i)$, where $i = \sqrt{-1}$?
    A) 6
    B) -2
    C) $6 - 4i\sqrt{2}$
    D) $2\sqrt{2} - 4i$

23. Which of the following is equivalent to $\frac{4}{2-3i}$, where $i = \sqrt{-1}$?
    A) $\frac{8}{13} - \frac{12}{13}i$
    B) $\frac{8}{13} + \frac{12}{13}i$
    C) $\frac{16}{13}$
    D) $-4i$

24. Which of the following is equivalent to $\frac{2-i}{3+4i}$, where $i = \sqrt{-1}$?
    A) $\frac{2}{7} - \frac{11}{7}i$
    B) $\frac{2}{7} + \frac{11}{7}i$
    C) $\frac{2}{25} - \frac{11}{25}i$
    D) $\frac{2}{5} + \frac{11}{25}i$

25. Which of the following is equivalent to $\frac{5+4i}{5-4i}$, where $i = \sqrt{-1}$?
    A) $\frac{9}{41} + \frac{40}{41}i$
    B) $\frac{9}{41} - \frac{40}{41}i$
    C) $1 - \frac{40}{9}i$
    D) $1 + \frac{40}{9}i$

$$x^2 = 2$$

26. Which of the following are solutions to the equation above?
    I. $x = 2$
    II. $x = \sqrt{2}$
    III. $x = -\sqrt{2}$

    A) I only
    B) II only
    C) II and III
    D) I, II, and III

$$(x+a)(x-b) = 0$$

27. Which of the following are solutions to the equation above?
    A) $x = a, b$
    B) $x = a, -b$
    C) $x = -a, b$
    D) $x = -a, -b$

28. Determine the solutions to the equation
$$x^2 - 7x + 10 = 0$$

29. Determine the solutions to the equation
$$x^2 + 5x - 24 = 0$$

30. Determine the solutions to the equation
$$x^2 + 14x + 49 = 0$$

31. Determine the solutions to the equation
$$2x^2 - 7x - 4 = 0$$

32. Determine the solutions to the equation
$$4x^2 - 9 = 0$$

33. Determine the solutions to the equation
$$3x^2 - 4x - 8 = 2x^2 + 4$$

34. Determine the solutions to the equation
$$2x^2 + 3 = 9 - x$$

35. Determine the solutions to the equation
$$3x^2 + 2x + 7 = 12x - 2x^2 + 7$$

36. Determine the solutions to the equation
$$x^2 - 5x + 5 = 0$$

37. Determine the solutions to the equation
$$x^2 + x - 1 = 0$$

38. Determine the solutions to the equation
$$2x^2 - 5x + 3 = 0$$

39. Determine the solutions to the equation
$$x^2 + x + 1 = 0$$

40. Determine the solutions to the equation
$$3x^2 - 2x + 1 = 0$$

Consider the equation

$$ax^2 + bx + c = 0$$

where a, b, and c are real constants. The solutions to the equation are given by the quadratic formula

$$x = \frac{-b \pm \sqrt{b^2 - 4ac}}{2a}$$

41. If $b^2 - 4ac > 0$ in the equation above, how many distinct real values x are solutions to the equation?
    A) Zero
    B) One
    C) Two
    D) More than two

42. If $b^2 - 4ac = 0$ in the equation above, how many distinct real values x are solutions to the equation?
    A) Zero
    B) One
    C) Two
    D) More than two

43. If $b^2 - 4ac < 0$ in the equation above, how many distinct real values x are solutions to the equation?
    A) Zero
    B) One
    C) Two
    D) More than two

$$2x^2 - 7x + 6 = 0$$

44. How many distinct real values x are solutions to the above equation?

$$5x^2 + 2x = 8$$

45. How many distinct real values x are solutions to the above equation?

$$3x^2 + 4x - 9 = 8x - 3$$

46. How many distinct real values x are solutions to the above equation?

$$4x^2 - 8x + t = 0$$

47. If $t = 4$ in the equation above, how many real distinct values x are solutions to the above equation?
    A) Zero
    B) One
    C) Two
    D) More than two

48. If the above equation has two real solutions x, which of the following could be the value of t?
    A) 3
    B) 4
    C) 5
    D) 6

49. If the above equation has no real solutions x, which of the following could be the value of t?
    A) -3
    B) 0
    C) 3
    D) 6

$$3x^2 + 10 = tx$$

50. If $t = 8$ in the equation above, how many real distinct values x are solutions to the above equation?
    A) Zero
    B) One
    C) Two
    D) More than two

51. If the above equation has no real solutions x, which of the following CANNOT be the value of t?
    A) -4
    B) 0
    C) 7
    D) 11

$$x^2 + (t+2)x + t + 3 = 0$$

52. If the above equation has two real solutions, which of the following is the best representation for the possible values of t?
    A) $|t| > 8$
    B) $|t| > 2\sqrt{2}$
    C) $|t| < 8$
    D) $|t| < 2\sqrt{2}$

53. The graph of $y = x^2 - 2x - 3$ is a parabola in the xy-plane. In which of the following equations do the x-coordinate and y-coordinate of the vertex of the parabola appear as constants or coefficients?
    A) $y = (x-1)(x+3)$
    B) $y = (x-3)(x+1)$
    C) $y = (x-1)^2 - 4$
    D) $y = x(x-2) - 3$

54. The graph of $y = x^2 - 2x - 3$ is a parabola in the xy-plane. In which of the following equations do the x-intercepts of the parabola appear as constants or coefficients?
    A) $y = (x-2)(x+3)$
    B) $y = (x-3)(x+1)$
    C) $y = (x-1)^2 - 4$
    D) $y = x(x-2) - 3$

55. Determine the x-intercepts of the graph of $y = -x^2 - 6x - 8$

56. Determine the vertex of the graph of $y = -x^2 - 6x - 8$

57. Determine the x-intercepts of the graph of the equation $y = 3x^2 - 6x$ in the xy-plane.

58. Determine the vertex of the graph of the equation $y = 3x^2 - 6x$ in the xy-plane.

59. Determine the x-intercepts of the graph of the equation $y = -2x^2 + 12x - 10$ in the xy-plane.

60. Determine the vertex of the graph of the equation $y = -2x^2 + 12x - 10$ in the xy-plane.

61. The graph of a parabola in the xy-plane has x-intercepts $(-2, 0)$ and $(8, 0)$. Determine the x-coordinate of the vertex of the parabola.

62. The graph of a parabola in the xy-plane passes through two points $(3, 5)$ and $(10, 5)$. Determine the x-coordinate of the vertex of the parabola.

63. The graph of a parabola in the xy-plane has an x-intercept $(-3, 0)$ and vertex $(-5, 8)$. Determine the other x-intercept of the parabola.

64. Determine the sum of the x-intercepts of the graph of the equation $y = x^2 + 4x - 21$.

65. Determine the sum of the x-intercepts of the graph of the equation $y = 2x^2 + 5x - 12$.

66. Determine the sum of the x-intercepts of the graph of the equation $y = -x^2 + 6x + 13$.

67. Determine the sum of the x-intercepts of the graph of the equation $y = ax^2 + bx + c$ if a, b, and c are constants. Once you find this result re-do questions 64, 65, and 66. You will find this formula in the SAT & ACT Facts and Formulas Section.

4.5 Radicals and Quadratic Equations Part 2

1. Determine the solutions to the equation
$$x^2 + 3x - 8 = 2x - 2$$

2. Determine the solutions to the equation
$$2x^2 - 5x = 3x + 8$$

$$y = x^2 + 5x + 2$$
$$y = 8x + 6$$

3. Determine the ordered pairs (x, y) that satisfy the system of equations above.

$$y = x^2 + 9x + 4$$
$$y = 3x^2 + 4x + 1$$

4. Determine the ordered pairs (x, y) that satisfy the system of equations above.

5. Determine the x-coordinates of the intersections of the parabola $y = x^2 - 7x + 10$ and the line $y = -2$.

6. Determine the x-coordinates of the intersections of the parabola $y = x^2 + 5x + 14$ and the line $y = -3x + 2$.

7. Determine the number of distinct real values x that are solutions to the equation
$$x^2 + 7x + 2 = -2x + 5$$

8. Determine the number of intersections of the parabola $y = -x^2 + 5x + 12$ and the line $y = 2x - 3$.

9. Determine the number of intersections of the parabola $y = x^2 - 3x + 8$ and the line $y = x - 4$.

10. Determine the number of intersections of the parabola $y = x^2 - 7x + 12$ and the line $y = x - 4$.

11. Determine the number of intersections of the parabola $y = 2x^2 + 5x - 8$ and the parabola $y = x^2 - 2x + 4$.

12. Determine the number of intersections of the parabola $y = x^2 + 7x - 12$ and the parabola $y = x^2 - 3x + 14$.

$$y = 2x^3 - 5x^2 + 8x - 4$$
$$y = 2x^3 + 4x^2 + x - 21$$

13. Determine the number of ordered pairs (x, y) that satisfy the system of equations above.

14. Which of the following is equivalent to $(a+b)^2$?
    A) $a^2 + b^2$
    B) $a^2 + ab + b^2$
    C) $a^2 + 2ab + b^2$
    D) $a^2 b^2$

15. Which of the following is equivalent to $(a-b)^2$?
    A) $a^2 - b^2$
    B) $a^2 - ab + b^2$
    C) $a^2 - 2ab + b^2$
    D) $a^2 b^2$

16. Which of the following is equivalent to $a^2 - b^2$?
    A) $(a+b)^2$
    B) $(a-b)^2$
    C) $(a-b)(a-b)$
    D) $(a+b)(a-b)$

17. Which of the following is equivalent to $(a+b)^2 + (a-b)^2$?
    A) $2a^2$
    B) $4ab$
    C) $2(a^2 + b^2)$
    D) 0

18. Which of the following is equivalent to $(a+b)^2 - (a-b)^2$?
    A) $2a^2$
    B) $4ab$
    C) $2(a^2 + b^2)$
    D) 0

19. Which of the following is equivalent to $\frac{a^2-16}{a-4}$?
    A) $a + 4$
    B) $a - 4$
    C) a
    D) 4

20. Which of the following is equivalent to $\frac{25-4a^2}{2a+5}$?
    A) $2a - 5$
    B) $2a + 5$
    C) $-2a + 5$
    D) $5a - 2$

21. Which of the following is equivalent to $\frac{18-2a^2}{a-3}$?
    A) $a + 3$
    B) $a - 3$
    C) $-2a - 3$
    D) $-2a - 6$

22. If $a^2 + b^2 = 15$ and $a + b = 3$, what is the value of ab?

23. If $a^2 + b^2 = 18$ and $a - b = -4$, what is the value of ab?

24. If $a^2 + b^2 = 11$ and $ab = 1$, what is the value of $a - b$?

25. If $ab = -5$ and $a + b = -5$, what is the value of $a^2 + b^2$?

26. If $a^2 - b^2 = 8$ and $a + b = -2$, what is the value of $a - b$?

27. If $a^2 - b^2 = -12$ and $a - b = 4$, what is the value of $a + b$?

28. If $3a^2 - 3b^2 = -15$ and $a + b = 1$, what is the value of $b - a$?

29. The expression $4x^2 - 25$ can be rewritten as
$$(px+q)(px-q)$$
where p and q are positive constants.

Which of the following could be the value of p in the expression above?
A) 4
B) 2
C) 1
D) 0

30. Which of the following could be the value of q in the question above?
A) 25
B) 5
C) 1
D) 0

31. The expression $5x^2 - 16$ can be rewritten as
$$(px+q)(px-q)$$
where p and q are positive constants.

Which of the following could be the value of p in the expression above?
A) 25
B) 5
C) $\sqrt{5}$
D) 0

32. Which of the following could be the value of q in the expression above?
A) 16
B) -4
C) -2
D) 1

33. The expression $\frac{1}{4}x^2 - 9$ can be rewritten as
$$(px+q)(px-q)$$
where p and q are positive constants.

Which of the following could be the value of p?
A) $\frac{1}{4}$
B) $-\frac{1}{4}$
C) $\frac{1}{2}$
D) $-\frac{1}{2}$

34. Determine the value of q in the expression above.

35. The expression $4x^2 - 25$ can be rewritten as
$$4(x+k)(x-k)$$
where k is a positive constant.

Which of the following could be the value of k in the expression above?
A) 5
B) $\frac{25}{4}$
C) $\frac{5}{2}$
D) $-\frac{5}{2}$

36. The expression $\frac{1}{4}x^2 - 16$ can be rewritten as
$$\frac{1}{4}(x+k)(x-k)$$
where k is a positive constant.

Which of the following could be the value of k?
A) 8
B) 4
C) 2
D) $\frac{1}{2}$

37. The expression $\frac{1}{3}x^2 - 2$ can be rewritten as
$$\frac{1}{3}(x+k)(x-k)$$
where k is a positive constant.

Which of the following could be the value of k in the expression above?
A) $\sqrt{6}$
B) $\sqrt{2}$
C) $\sqrt{\frac{2}{3}}$
D) 2

38. The expression $\frac{2}{3}x^2 - \frac{3}{8}$ can be rewritten as
$$\frac{2}{3}(x+k)(x-k)$$
where k is a positive constant.

Determine the value of k.

34

Consider the system of equations
$$x^2 + y^2 = p$$
$$xy = q$$
where p and q are real constants.

39. Which of the following is equivalent to the expression $2(x+y)^2$?
    A) $2p + 2q$
    B) $2p + 4q$
    C) $2p$
    D) $2q^2$

40. Which of the following is equivalent to the expression $(2x - 2y)^2$?
    A) $2p - 2q$
    B) $4p - 8q$
    C) $p^2 - q^2$
    D) $2q^2$

41. Which of the following is equivalent to the expression $x + y$?
    A) $\sqrt{p}$
    B) $\sqrt{p-q}$
    C) $\sqrt{p+2q}$
    D) $2\sqrt{q}$

Consider the system of equations
$$x^2 - y^2 = p$$
$$x - y = q$$
where p and q are real constants.

42. Which of the following is equivalent to the expression $3x + 3y$?
    A) $3q$
    B) $3\sqrt{p}$
    C) $\frac{3p}{q}$
    D) $3(p - q^2)$

43. Which of the following is equivalent to x?
    A) $\frac{p+q^2}{2q}$
    B) $\frac{\sqrt{p}+q}{2}$
    C) $\frac{\sqrt{p+q^2}}{2}$
    D) $\sqrt{\frac{p+q^2}{2}}$

$$y = kx^2 - a$$

In the equation above, k and a are constants with $k < 0$ and $a > 0$.

44. Which of the following correctly describes the graph of the equation above in the xy-plane?
    A) Parabola with vertex $(0, a)$ that opens upward
    B) Parabola with vertex $(0, a)$ that opens downward
    C) Parabola with vertex $(0, -a)$ that opens upward
    D) Parabola with vertex $(0, -a)$ that opens downward

45. Which of the following is an equivalent form of the equation above?
    A) $k(x + \sqrt{a})(x - \sqrt{a})$
    B) $\sqrt{k}(x + \sqrt{a})(x - \sqrt{a})$
    C) $(kx + \sqrt{a})(kx - \sqrt{a})$
    D) $k(x + \sqrt{\frac{a}{k}})(x - \sqrt{\frac{a}{k}})$

46. If $(b, 0)$ and $(c, 0)$ are the x-intercepts of the graph of the equation above in the xy-plane, which of the following is value of $b + c$?
    A) 0
    B) a
    C) $2a$
    D) $2\sqrt{\frac{a}{k}}$

$$y = k(x - a)^2$$

In the equation above, k and a are constants with $k > 0$ and $a < 0$.

47. Which of the following correctly describes the graph of the equation above in the xy-plane?
    A) Parabola with vertex $(a, 0)$ that opens upward
    B) Parabola with vertex $(a, 0)$ that opens downward
    C) Parabola with vertex $(-a, 0)$ that opens upward
    D) Parabola with vertex $(-a, 0)$ that opens downward

48. If $(b, 0)$ and $(c, 0)$ are the x-intercepts of the graph of the equation above in the xy-plane, which of the following is value of $b + c$?
    A) 0
    B) a
    C) $2a$
    D) $-2a$

49. Determine the distance between the point $(3,4)$ in the xy-plane and the origin.

50. Determine the distance between the points $(7,2)$ and $(10,6)$ in the xy-plane.

51. If the line segment connecting the points $(-3,-5)$ and $(5,1)$ is the diameter of a circle in the xy-plane, determine the radius of the circle.

Recall that a circle is the set of all the points at a distance r from the center. The equation of a circle in the xy-plane with its center at the origin and radius r is therefore
$$\sqrt{x^2 + y^2} = r$$
which is more commonly written as
$$x^2 + y^2 = r^2$$

52. Determine the radius of the circle given by the equation $x^2 + y^2 = 16$.

53. Determine the radius of the circle given by the equation $3x^2 + 3y^2 = 12$.

54. Determine the radius of the circle given by the equation $\frac{2}{3}x^2 + \frac{2}{3}y^2 = 24$.

55. Determine the radius of the circle given by the equation $4x^2 + 4y^2 = 25$.

If a circle in the xy-plane has center (h,k), and radius r then the equation of the circle is found by setting the distance between (x,y) and (h,k) equal to r:
$$(x-h)^2 + (y-k)^2 = r^2$$

Consider a circle in the xy-plane given by the equation:
$$x^2 + 6x + y^2 - 4y = 3$$

56. Determine the coordinates (x,y) of the center of the circle given by the equation above.

57. Determine the radius of the circle given by the equation above.

Consider a circle in the xy-plane given by the equation
$$2x^2 - 8x + 2y^2 - 4y = -8$$

58. Determine the coordinates (x,y) of the center of the circle given by the equation above.

59. Determine the radius of the circle given by the equation above.

Consider a circle in the xy-plane given by the equation
$$4x^2 + 12x + 4y^2 - 20y = 15$$

60. Determine the coordinates (x,y) of the center of the circle given by the equation above.

61. Determine the radius of the circle given by the equation above.

4.6 Exponents and Radicals

1. Which of the following is equivalent to x^{a+b}?
   A) $x^a + x^b$
   B) $x^a \cdot x^b$
   C) $ax + bx$
   D) x^{ab}

2. Which of the following is equivalent to x^{ab}?
   A) $x^a + x^b$
   B) $x^a \cdot x^b$
   C) x^{a^b}
   D) $(x^b)^a$

3. Which of the following is equivalent to x^{-a}?
   A) $-x^a$
   B) $(-x)^a$
   C) $\frac{1}{x^a}$
   D) $\sqrt[a]{x}$

4. Which of the following is equivalent to $x^{1/a}$?
   A) x^{-a}
   B) $\frac{1}{x^a}$
   C) $\frac{1}{a^x}$
   D) $\sqrt[a]{x}$

5. Which of the following is equivalent to $x^{a/b}$?
   A) $\sqrt[a]{x^b}$
   B) $\sqrt[b]{x^a}$
   C) $\frac{x^a}{x^b}$
   D) x^{a-b}

6. Which of the following is equivalent to $\frac{(x^2 y^{-3})^4}{x^7 y^{-10}}$?
   A) $x^{15} y^2$
   B) $\frac{y^3}{x}$
   C) $\frac{x}{y^2}$
   D) xy^2

7. Which of the following is equivalent to $\frac{(x^{2/3} y^{-1/4})^3}{(x^{-1/3} y^{3/4})^2}$?
   A) $\frac{x^2 \sqrt[3]{x^2}}{y^2 \sqrt[4]{y}}$
   B) $\frac{x^2 \sqrt[3]{x}}{y^2 \sqrt[4]{y}}$
   C) $\frac{x^2 \sqrt[3]{x^2}}{y^2 \sqrt[4]{y^3}}$
   D) $\frac{x^2 \sqrt[3]{x}}{y^2 \sqrt[4]{y^3}}$

8. Which of the following is equivalent to $8^{2/3}$?
   A) 4
   B) $\frac{64}{3}$
   C) $\frac{16}{3}$
   D) 12

9. Which of the following is equivalent to $9^{1/4}$?
   A) 3
   B) $\sqrt{3}$
   C) $\sqrt[4]{3}$
   D) $\sqrt{9^4}$

10. Which of the following is equivalent to $2^{3/2}$?
    A) $\sqrt{2}$
    B) $\sqrt[3]{4}$
    C) $2\sqrt{2}$
    D) 3

11. Which of the following is equivalent to $\left(\frac{9}{4}\right)^{1/2}$?
    A) $\frac{9}{8}$
    B) $\frac{3}{2}$
    C) $\frac{4}{9}$
    D) $\frac{16}{81}$

12. Which of the following is equivalent to $\left(\frac{9}{4}\right)^{-1/2}$?
    A) $-\frac{4}{9}$
    B) $-\frac{3}{2}$
    C) $\frac{2}{3}$
    D) $\frac{16}{81}$

13. Which of the following is equivalent to $(-8)^{2/3}$?
    A) -4
    B) 4
    C) $-4\sqrt{2}$
    D) This expression cannot be evaluated.

14. Which of the following is equivalent to $8^{3/2}$?
    A) 256
    B) $16\sqrt{2}$
    C) 16
    D) $8\sqrt{2}$

15. Which of the following is equivalent to 2^{-x}?
    A) -2^x
    B) $(-2)^x$
    C) $\sqrt{x}$
    D) $\left(\frac{1}{2}\right)^x$

16. Which of the following is equivalent to 2^{3x}?
    A) 6^x
    B) 8^x
    C) 3^{2x}
    D) 2^{x^3}

17. Which of the following is equivalent to 2^{4-2x}?
    A) $8 - 4x$
    B) $16 - 4^x$
    C) $\frac{4}{x}$
    D) $\frac{16}{4^x}$

18. Which of the following is equivalent to $\frac{16^x}{2^{3x}}$?
    A) 8^{-2x}
    B) 8^x
    C) 2^x
    D) $\frac{8}{2^x}$

19. Which of the following is equivalent to $\frac{3^{2x}}{9^{x+1}}$?
    A) 1
    B) $\frac{1}{9}$
    C) 3^{x-1}
    D) 9^{x-1}

20. Which of the following is equivalent to $\frac{3^{2x-1}}{9^{x-2}}$?
    A) 27
    B) 9
    C) 3
    D) 1

21. Which of the following is equivalent to $\frac{4^{2-x}}{2^{-2x}}$?
    A) 16
    B) 8
    C) 4
    D) 2

22. If $x = y + 2$, what is the value of $\frac{2^x}{2^y}$?
    A) 2
    B) 4
    C) x^2
    D) 2^x

23. If $2x - y = 3$, what is the value of $\frac{4^{x-2}}{2^y}$?
    A) $\frac{1}{4}$
    B) $\frac{1}{2}$
    C) 2
    D) 4

24. If $3x - 2y = 4$, what is the value of $\frac{8^x}{4^y}$?
    A) 2^4
    B) 4
    C) 2
    D) 2^x

25. If $\frac{4^{a^2}}{4^{b^2}} = 16$, which of the following is equivalent to $a^2 - b^2$?
    A) 16
    B) 4
    C) 2
    D) 1

26. If $\frac{x^{a^2}}{x^{b^2}} = x^8$, which of the following is equivalent to $a^2 - b^2$?
    A) x^8
    B) 8
    C) 1
    D) 0

27. If $\frac{x^{a^2}}{x^{b^2}} = x^{12}$ and $a + b = 4$, what is the value of $a - b$?
    A) 12
    B) 4
    C) 3
    D) 1

28. If $\frac{3^{2a}}{9^b} = 81$ and $a^2 - b^2 = 6$, what is the value of $a + b$?
    A) 81
    B) 12
    C) 6
    D) 3

A population of rabbits doubles every 15 years. The rabbit population was 4,000 in 2008.

29. Which of the following could represent P, the population of rabbits, in terms of t, the number of years after 2008?
    A) $P = 4000 \cdot 2^{15t}$
    B) $P = 4000 \cdot 2^{t/15}$
    C) $P = 4000 \cdot 15^{2t}$
    D) $P = 15 \cdot 4000^{2t}$

30. In what year will the population be 32,000?
    A) 2011
    B) 2023
    C) 2053
    D) 2128

31. In what year was the population 1,000?
    A) 1948
    B) 1963
    C) 1978
    D) 1993

A radioactive substance has a half life of 40 min. The amount of substance will decay exponentially such that it will lose half of its remaining amount every 40 minutes.

32. How long will it take for 200 g of this substance to decay to 50 g?
    A) 20 minutes
    B) 40 minutes
    C) 80 minutes
    D) 120 minutes

33. If a sample of this substance currently has 42 g remaining, how much of the substance was present in the sample 80 minutes ago?
    A) 21 g
    B) 42 g
    C) 84 g
    D) 168 g

34. Which of the following could represent R, the remaining amount of the substance, in terms of R_0, the initial amount of the substance, and t, the time elapsed in minutes?
    A) $R = R_0 \cdot 2^{40t}$
    B) $R = R_0 \cdot 2^{t/40}$
    C) $R = R_0 \cdot 2^{-40t}$
    D) $R = R_0 \cdot 2^{-t/40}$

The population of a certain city increases by 3% every year. The population of the city was 185,000 in 1965.

35. Which of the following could represent P, the population of this city, in terms of t, the number of years after 1965?
    A) $P = 185,000(3)^t$
    B) $P = 185,000(0.03)^t$
    C) $P = 185,000(1.03)^t$
    D) $P = (185,000 \cdot 0.03)^t$

36. The population of this city in 1982 was what percent greater than its population in 1981?
    A) 2.9%
    B) 3.0%
    C) 3.1%
    D) 3.2%

37. The population of this city in 1992 was what percent greater than its population in 1988?
    A) 3.0%
    B) 4.0%
    C) 12.0%
    D) 12.6%

A bacterial colony exposed to a particular chemical will decrease in size by 25% every minute. 7.2 million members were present in the colony when first exposed to the chemical.

38. Which of the following could represent P, the population of the bacteria colony in millions, in terms of t, the number of minutes elapsed since the colony was first exposed to the chemical?
    A) $P = 7.2(25)^t$
    B) $P = 7.2(0.25)^t$
    C) $P = 7.2(0.75)^t$
    D) $P = 7.2(1.25)^t$

39. Which of the following represents the number change in the number of bacteria **during the third minute** (this wording means "from $t = 2$ to $t = 3$") since exposure?
    A) $7.2(0.75^3 - 0.75^2)$
    B) $7.2(0.75)$
    C) $7.2(0.75^2 - 0.75^3)$
    D) $\frac{7.2}{0.75}$

Amy has discovered an investment with an 8% interest rate, compounded quarterly. She invests $5,000.

The following model represents V, the account value in dollars, in terms of t, the number of years after the initial investment.

$$V = P\left(1 + \frac{r}{n}\right)^{nt}$$

40. In the model above, what is the value of P?
    A) 4
    B) 8
    C) 0.08
    D) 5,000

41. In the model above, what is the value of n?
    A) 4
    B) 8
    C) 0.08
    D) 5,000

42. In the model above, what is the value of r?
    A) 4
    B) 8
    C) 0.08
    D) 5,000

The scenario below is a continuation of the previous scenario.

Beth has discovered a similar investment with a 6% interest rate, compounded quarterly. She invests $5,000 at the same time Amy makes her initial investment.

43. Which of the following represents the difference in the values of Amy and Beth's investments after two years?
    A) $5,000[(1.02)^8 - (1.015)^8]$
    B) $5,000[(1.08)^8 - (1.06)^8]$
    C) $5,000(0.005)^8$
    D) $5,000(0.02)^8$

44. Which of the following represents the ratio of Amy's account value to Beth's account value after three years?
    A) $5,000\left(\frac{1.02}{1.015}\right)^{12}$
    B) $5,000\left(\frac{1.08}{1.06}\right)^{12}$
    C) $\left(\frac{1.02}{1.015}\right)^{12}$
    D) $\left(\frac{1.08}{1.06}\right)^{12}$

The table below gives some value for a continuous function f.

x	0	1	2	3
$f(x)$	3	6	12	24

45. According to the table above, which of the following could represent f?
    A) $f(x) = 3x$
    B) $f(x) = 3x^2$
    C) $f(x) = 3^x$
    D) $f(x) = 3 \cdot 2^x$

x	0	1	2	3	4
$f(x)$	4	3	$\frac{9}{4}$	$\frac{27}{16}$	$\frac{81}{64}$

46. According to the table above, which of the following could represent f?
    A) $f(x) = 4 - x$
    B) $f(x) = \frac{4}{x}$
    C) $f(x) = 4 \cdot \left(\frac{3}{4}\right)^x$
    D) $f(x) = 4 \cdot \left(\frac{9}{4}\right)^x$

x	1	2	3	4	5
$f(x)$	16	8	4	2	1

47. According to the table above, which of the following could represent f?
    A) $f(x) = 32 \cdot 2^{-x}$
    B) $f(x) = 16 \cdot 2^{-x}$
    C) $f(x) = 16 \cdot \left(\frac{1}{2}\right)^x$
    D) $f(x) = \frac{16}{x}$

x	0	2	4	6
$f(x)$	8	18	$\frac{81}{2}$	$\frac{729}{8}$

48. According to the table above, which of the following could represent f?
    A) $f(x) = 8 \cdot \left(\frac{9}{2}\right)^x$
    B) $f(x) = 8 \cdot \left(\frac{9}{4}\right)^x$
    C) $f(x) = 8 \cdot \left(\frac{3}{2}\right)^x$
    D) $f(x) = 8 \cdot \left(\frac{9}{4}\right)^{2x}$

5 SAT + ACT Packet Answers

Following are the Answers to the 6 Practice Sections.

5.1 Linear Equations Answers

1. C) The stalk was 8.1 centimeters tall when the student began observing.

2. A) The stalk grew 2.7 centimeters each day.

3. D) 35

4. B) $d = \frac{h-8.1}{2.7}$

5. B) 7

6. Price of renting the car increases $0.40 per mile.

7. Base price for renting the car is $18.

8. $46

9. $m = \frac{p-18}{0.4}$

10. 152 miles

11. $y = 2x$

12. $y = -x + 2$

13. $y = \frac{1}{2}x - 3$

14.

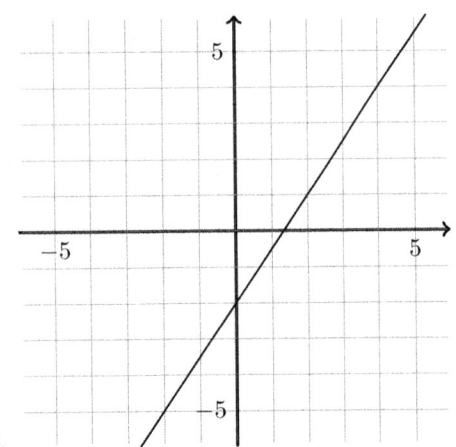

15.

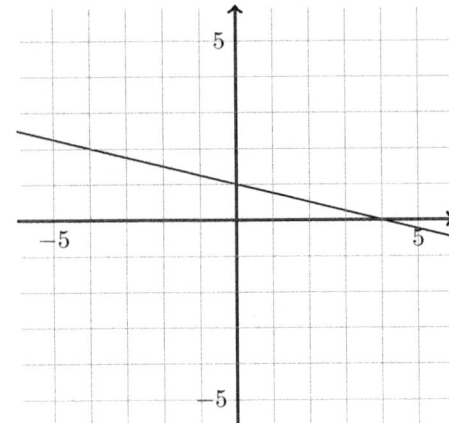

16.

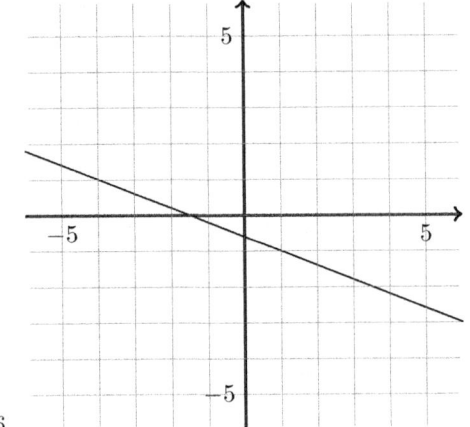

17. D) $\frac{-3}{5}$

18. A) 2

19. B) $\frac{10}{3}$

20. C) $(\frac{3}{5}, 3)$

21. $\frac{-2}{3}$

22. 2

23. 3

24. $\frac{8}{3}$

25. $(0, 5)$

26. $(\frac{-15}{8}, 0)$

27. B) $(-3, -3)$

28. $\frac{-a}{b}$

29. $(0, \frac{c}{b})$

30. $(\frac{c}{a}, 0)$

31. D) IV

32. C) III

33. A) I

34. B) II

35. B) II

36. C) The slope of line l is positive.

37. D) The y-intercept of line l is negative.

38. C) $a < 0, b > 0$

39. B) $y = \frac{2}{5}x + 3$

40. C) $y = -\frac{5}{2}x + 4$

41. C) $3x - 12y = 9$

42. C) $12x + 3y = -1$

43. A) $x + 2y = 4$

44. C) $4x - 2y + 9 = 0$

45. C) $ax - by = -c$

46. B) $2x + y = 4$

5.2 Inequalities and Systems of Equations Answers

1. A) $x = -1$
2. D) $x = -4$ is not a solution.
3. C) $x > -3$
4. D) $x = 2$
5. B) $x \leq 2$
6. D) $x = 2$ is not a solution.
7. A) $x > 2$ or $x < 0$
8. $x > \dfrac{-3}{5}$
9. $2 < x < \dfrac{10}{3}$
10. $-2 < x \leq \dfrac{-7}{4}$
11. B) $(0, 2)$ is a solution.
12. C) $y > \dfrac{3}{2}x - 3$
13. D) $x < \dfrac{8}{3}$
14. C) $(2, -5)$ is not a solution.
15. A) $(0, 0)$
16. $y > 3x + 6$
17. $x < \dfrac{y}{3} - 2$
18. $y > 3$
19. $x < \dfrac{-4}{3}$
20. $y \leq \dfrac{-a}{b}x + \dfrac{c}{b}$
21. $x \geq \dfrac{-b}{a}y + \dfrac{c}{a}$
22. $y \geq \dfrac{-5a}{b} + \dfrac{c}{b}$
23. $y \leq \dfrac{-2}{b} + \dfrac{c}{b}$
24. D) $y < 2x - 3$
25. C) $(2, 0)$ is a solution.

26.

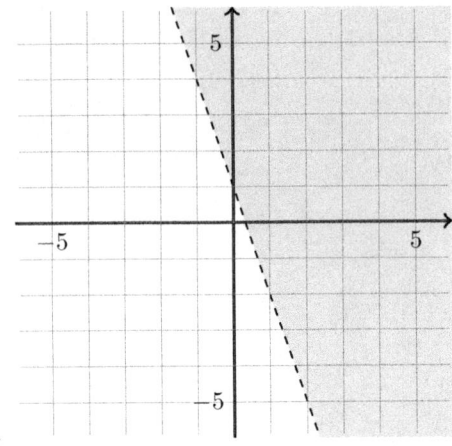

27. C) $3y + x \geq 6$
28. B) $(2, 1)$ is not a solution

29.

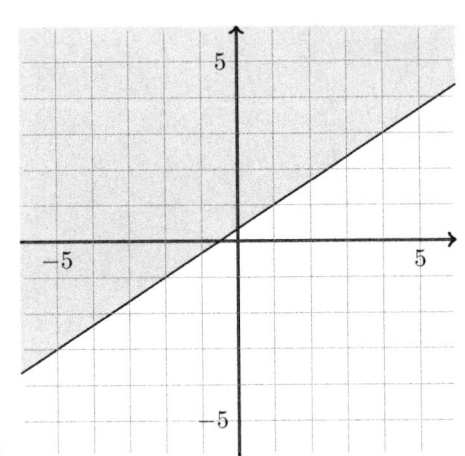

30. B) $(2, 4)$ is a solution.
31. C) 6
32. $(1, -3)$
33. 5
34. 1
35. 2
36. -1
37. -5
38. $\dfrac{2}{3}$
39. -7
40. A) Zero

41. B) One

42. D) More than two

43. B) One

44. D) More than two

45. A) Zero

46. $a = -3$, $b = 8$

47. $a = 4$, $b = 6$

48. C) 0

49. B) $\dfrac{-2}{3}$

50. B) $y > -x + 3$ and $y \geq 2x - 4$

51. C) $(2, 1)$

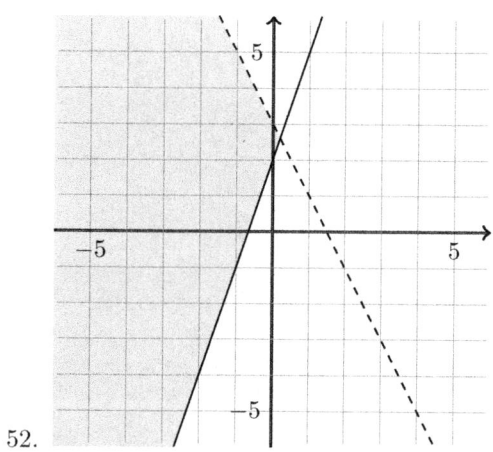

52.

53. A) $a < b$

54. A) $a < b$

55. D) $b = 0$

45

5.3 Ratios and Probability Answers

1. D) 21
2. B) $\frac{3}{4}$
3. C) $\frac{5}{2}$
4. D) 4
5. A) 2
6. A) 2
7. B) $\frac{1}{2}$
8. 80 minutes
9. 1.2 hours or 1 hour and 12 minutes
10. $2\frac{2}{3}$ cups powder sugar
11. 360 milliliters
12. 24 marbles
13. B) $y = 0.3x$
14. D) $y = 1.4x$
15. D) $y = 0.75x$
16. C) $D = 0.05a + 0.08b$
17. A) $R = \frac{0.05a + 0.08b}{a+b}$
18. C) $(1.08)(0.76)C$
19. D) $\frac{p}{(1.08)(0.83)}$
20. B) $\frac{0.24C + 0.17E}{C+E}$
21. D) 14
22. C) 24%
23. A) 14%
24. B) 76%
25. C) 62%
26. C) 74%
27. D) 39%
28. B) 29%
29. 66
30. 42
31. 18
32. 90
33. 24
34. 6
35. 100%
36. 300%
37. D) $\frac{1}{2}$
38. B) $\frac{1}{4}$
39. C) $\frac{3}{4}$
40. A) $\frac{1}{36}$
41. B) $\frac{1}{9}$
42. $\frac{1}{2}$
43. $\frac{1}{13}$
44. $\frac{25}{52}$
45. $\frac{27}{52}$
46. $\frac{1}{4}$
47. $\frac{1}{36}$
48. D) $\frac{74}{152}$
49. C) $\frac{56}{152}$
50. B) $\frac{10}{45}$
51. C) $\frac{51}{74}$
52. $\frac{335}{731}$
53. $\frac{354}{731}$
54. $\frac{87}{731}$
55. $\frac{87}{321}$ or $\frac{29}{107}$
56. $\frac{18}{155}$

5.4 Radicals and Quadratic Equations Part 1 Answers

1. C) $x^2 + 2ax + a^2$
2. D) $x^2 - 2ax + a^2$
3. B) $x^2 - a^2$
4. D) $4a^2 - ab + \frac{b^2}{16}$
5. C) $a + b$
6. D) ab
7. D) -15
8. B) 3
9. C) 1
10. D) $-\frac{5}{2}$
11. D) $-\frac{3}{2}$
12. B) 5
13. B) 5
14. B) $2 + 3\sqrt{2}$
15. C) $5 + 2\sqrt{6}$
16. A) 11
17. B) $2\sqrt{3}$
18. D) $\frac{3}{2} + \frac{1}{2}\sqrt{5}$
19. A) $\frac{11}{7} - \frac{6}{7}\sqrt{2}$
20. C) $8 + 8i$
21. D) $7 - 24i$
22. A) 6
23. B) $\frac{8}{13} + \frac{12}{13}i$
24. C) $\frac{2}{25} - \frac{11}{25}i$
25. A) $\frac{9}{41} + \frac{40}{41}i$
26. C) II and III
27. C) $x = -a, b$
28. $x = 2, 5$
29. $x = 3, -8$
30. $x = -7$
31. $x = 4, -\frac{1}{2}$
32. $x = \pm\frac{3}{2}$
33. $x = 6, -2$
34. $x = \frac{3}{2}, -2$
35. $x = 0, 2$
36. $x = \frac{5 \pm \sqrt{5}}{2}$
37. $x = \frac{-1 \pm \sqrt{5}}{2}$
38. $x = 1, \frac{3}{2}$
39. $x = \frac{-1 \pm i\sqrt{3}}{2}$
40. $x = \frac{1 \pm i\sqrt{2}}{3}$
41. C) Two
42. B) One
43. A) Zero
44. Two
45. Two
46. Two
47. B) One
48. A) 3
49. D) 6
50. A) Zero
51. D) 11
52. B) $|t| > 2\sqrt{2}$
53. C) $y = (x-1)^2 - 4$
54. B) $y = (x-3)(x+1)$
55. $(-2, 0), (-4, 0)$
56. $(-3, 1)$
57. $(0, 0), (2, 0)$
58. $(1, -3)$
59. $(1, 0), (5, 0)$
60. $(3, 8)$
61. $x = 3$
62. $x = \frac{13}{2}$ or 6.5
63. $(-7, 0)$
64. -4
65. $\frac{-5}{2}$ or -2.5
66. 6
67. $\frac{-b}{a}$

5.5 Radicals and Quadratic Equations Part 2 Answers

1. $x = 2, -3$
2. $x = 2 \pm 2\sqrt{2}$
3. $(4, 38), (-1, -2)$
4. $(3, 40), (-\frac{1}{2}, -\frac{1}{4})$
5. $x = 3, 4$
6. $x = -2, -6$
7. Two
8. Two
9. Zero
10. One
11. Two
12. One
13. Two
14. C) $a^2 + 2ab + b^2$
15. C) $a^2 - 2ab + b^2$
16. D) $(a+b)(a-b)$
17. C) $2(a^2 + b^2)$
18. B) $4ab$
19. A) $a + 4$
20. C) $-2a + 5$
21. D) $-2a - 6$
22. -3
23. 1
24. ± 3
25. 35
26. -4
27. -3
28. 5
29. B) 2
30. B) 5
31. C) $\sqrt{5}$
32. B) -4
33. C) $\frac{1}{2}$
34. 3
35. C) $\frac{5}{2}$
36. A) 8
37. A) $\sqrt{6}$
38. $\frac{3}{4}$
39. B) $2p + 4q$
40. B) $4p - 8q$
41. C) $\sqrt{p + 2q}$
42. C) $\frac{3p}{q}$
43. A) $\frac{p+q^2}{2q}$
44. D) Parabola with vertex $(0, -a)$ that opens downward
45. D) $k(x + \sqrt{\frac{a}{k}})(x - \sqrt{\frac{a}{k}})$
46. A) 0
47. A) Parabola with vertex $(a, 0)$ that opens upward
48. C) $2a$
49. 5
50. 5
51. 5
52. 4
53. 2
54. 6
55. $\frac{5}{2}$
56. $(-3, 2)$
57. 4
58. $(2, 1)$
59. 1
60. $(-\frac{3}{2}, \frac{5}{2})$
61. $\frac{7}{2}$

5.6 Exponents and Radicals Answers

1. B) $x^a \cdot x^b$
2. D) $(x^b)^a$
3. C) $\frac{1}{x^a}$
4. D) $\sqrt[a]{x}$
5. B) $\sqrt[b]{x^a}$
6. C) $\frac{x}{y^2}$
7. D) $\frac{x^2 \sqrt[3]{x^2}}{y^2 \sqrt[4]{y}}$
8. A) 4
9. B) $\sqrt{3}$
10. C) $2\sqrt{2}$
11. B) $\frac{3}{2}$
12. C) $\frac{2}{3}$
13. B) 4
14. B) $16\sqrt{2}$
15. D) $\left(\frac{1}{2}\right)^x$
16. B) 8^x
17. D) $\frac{16}{4^x}$
18. C) 2^x
19. B) $\frac{1}{9}$
20. A) 27
21. A) 16
22. B) 4
23. B) $\frac{1}{2}$
24. A) 2^4
25. C) 2
26. B) 8
27. C) 3
28. D) 3
29. B) $P = 4000 \cdot 2^{t/15}$
30. C) 2053
31. C) 1978
32. C) 80 minutes
33. D) 168 g
34. D) $R = R_0 \cdot 2^{-t/40}$
35. C) $P = 185,000(1.03)^t$
36. B) 3.0%
37. D) 12.6%
38. C) $P = 7.2(0.75)^t$
39. A) $7.2(0.75^3 - 0.75^2)$
40. D) 5,000
41. A) 4
42. C) 0.08
43. A) $5,000[(1.02)^8 - (1.015)^8]$
44. C) $\left(\frac{1.02}{1.015}\right)^{12}$
45. D) $f(x) = 3 \cdot 2^x$
46. C) $f(x) = 4 \cdot \left(\frac{3}{4}\right)^x$
47. A) $f(x) = 32 \cdot 2^{-x}$
48. C) $f(x) = 8 \cdot \left(\frac{3}{2}\right)^x$

Notes Page 1/3

Notes Page 2/3

Notes Page 3/3

Made in the USA
Las Vegas, NV
08 January 2021